THE COACHING COMPANION

Get the Most from Your Coaching Experience
2nd Edition

Carylynn Larson, PhD, PCC
Daniel Sheres, MPH, PCC

D1452794

2021
Alexandria, VA, USA

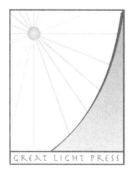

GREAT LIGHT PRESS

1

The Coaching Companion, 2nd Edition
Carylynn Larson and Daniel Sheres

Cover Design: Kariza Enriquez
Editor: Erin Greenwell

ISBN: 978-0-9861579-8-1
Version 2.0

Praise for *The Coaching Companion, 2ⁿᵈ Edition:*

"Coaching unlocks potential in individuals, enabling them to see possibilities for their lives, their careers and their organizations. The Coaching Companion provides useful information, examples and ideas for application in a practical and usable book. A "must read" for anyone who wants to create the best coaching partnership."

– Pat Mathews, MA, RN, MCC
Founding Faculty, Georgetown University Institute for Transformational Leadership

———————————

"The Coaching Companion is a gem of a book and a must-read for anyone seeking to get the absolute most out of their coaching relationship. Carylynn and Daniel have done a wonderful job of incorporating real-life examples, years of firsthand coaching experience and a deep understanding of what makes us each truly unique—as well as the ways in which we are all utterly the same. Into these practical tips and valuable suggestions is woven an honesty and authenticity that is refreshing, solidly grounded and tremendously helpful. Highly, highly recommended!"

– Chalmers Brothers
Author of *Language & the Pursuit of Happiness* and *Language & the Pursuit of Leadership Excellence*

"This book represents the culmination of years of work condensed into powerful insights that are perfect for anyone wanting to maximize a coaching experience. Whether you are just beginning or seek coaching regularly, you will benefit from the content and applications that Daniel and Carylynn have carefully thought out to ensure the successful integration of your experience."

– Brandon Moreno
Business Optimization Expert
President, EverHive

"Coaching has too often relied on the luck of connection rather than the science. The too long and often failed process of coach and client circling each other trying to land on connection is a failed and frustrating methodology. Finally we have a way for both coach and client to connect early and substantially for powerful, personal and productive outcomes on all sides. I have been an executive coach for nearly three decades and have not found a guide as simple, clear and useful as The Coaching Companion."

– Richard Godfrey
Chief Operating Officer/Chief Learning Officer
Life Engineering

Dedication

To the next generation of professionals, who will need to maximize every learning experience to lead us through the challenges facing our world. To everyone who coaches this next generation to growth and success.

Table of Contents

Foreword

Don Rheem, CEO, E3 Solutions

Author of *Thrive By Design: The Neuroscience That Drives High-Performance Cultures*

We all have biases, some known and some unconscious. I have a clear bias for science-based approaches to leadership because they are more reliable, replicable (in real life), and effective. Few books in the leadership and coaching genre explore with any depth the remarkable insights from the behavioral and neurosciences. One of the remarkable accomplishments of this title is how ably the authors have moved the coaching conversation from art to science. The Coaching Companion is practical, relevant, and has deep roots in empirically validated research in the behavioral sciences.

Why should you read this book? Two key reasons in my mind:

1. You want to understand the fundamental principles that create an effective coaching process.
2. You want to fine tune the process to maximize your experience and positive outcomes.

This book helps you accomplish both of these objectives. The Coaching Companion's endeavor to help you, the coachee, is a unique contribution to the literature and should not be underestimated.

I particularly appreciate the emphasis that this work places on:

Emotion: Homo sapiens are emotional, relational creatures at our core and any discussion of behavioral change, as these authors do, needs to show us how to use emotion productively. This advice permeates the entire book, much to its credit.

Self-Reflection: In the chapter, *Take Time to Reflect*, the authors note that "self-reflection is a critical pathway for personal growth." I could not agree more. The ability to better understand ourselves at a deeper level, they write, "enhances the perception of the learner and the relevance of what they are learning…and ultimately…improves work practices and performance."

Habits: Ultimately, a key goal of being coached is to change our habits so we can be more successful in the environments where we live and work. Habit change is exceedingly difficult for most of us, which is why readers don't want to miss the chapter, *Develop New Habits*. The reference to the role of rewards from a brain-based perspective, is particularly salient for anyone who wants to leave unsuccessful habits in favor of new ones that will propel them forward.

Authenticity: Over the years, countless managers have told me how hard it is to alter habits for fear of being seen as inauthentic or "faking it." Behavioral changes do not exist in a vacuum, everyone who interacts with you may notice what appears to be sudden shifts and behaviors (resulting from your coaching) and they'll want to understand what is driving these shifts. Can they be trusted? Are they authentic? What is the reason behind them? The authors explore this in the chapter, *Explain Your Change*, in a very practical and thorough way that I found unique and useful.

Mindfulness: Never before in our history have we experienced such complexity, stress, and social anxiety, both at work and at home. The additional metabolic load of doing work, of raising a family, just living, is much more intense than ever before. Tip 20, *Rejuvenate*, is particularly helpful in this regard, including the very thoughtful and practical discussions of the role of mindfulness and somatic awareness. And unlike the typical texts on creating work/life integration, the authors point out the seminal role of the emotional, mental, and physiological shifts that need to move in concert in order to maximize and solidify lasting behavioral change.

I have just highlighted a small representation of the salient, science-backed insights packed into *The Coaching Companion*. Additional chapters include helpful guidance on cultivating curiosity, how to visualize success, create clear coaching objectives, and translate insights into action, among others.

The coaching process is the most intimate within the larger "leadership development" field. It involves a one-on-one relationship with a coach, and to be successful the person being coached needs to reveal a great deal about their hopes, vulnerabilities, and habits. Navigating both the process and the coaching relationship can be challenging, and until this publication, there has been little advice to inform the coaching recipient on how to be an active participant. Here, you will learn how to manage your own change process (the epicenter of any great coaching experience), including how to identify the most important changes that will better position you for success in virtually any endeavor. The advice herein will exponentially improve your progress while being coached. Read it. Live it.

Don Rheem
CEO, E3 Solutions (E3Solutions.com)
Author of *Thrive By Design: The Neuroscience That Drives High-Performance Cultures* (Forbes | Books)

Introduction

Coaching is the process of helping someone get from where they are to where they want to be. Those who facilitate this process call themselves coaches, in a variety of domains. Beyond the everyday references to sports coaches, there are Leadership and Executive Coaches, Career Coaches, Health Coaches, Presentation Coaches, Relationship Coaches, and Life Coaches. Millions of people around the world leverage coaches to help them advance to the next level in their careers, elevate their skill sets, overcome challenges, leverage setbacks, navigate important relationships, improve their wellbeing, and realize their dreams.

When you invest in a coach, you're investing in a personalized program for growth (often referred to as a Coaching Engagement), which occurs over a timeframe that aligns with your goals—often 6 months to a year in duration. Your Coaching Engagement is likely to include meetings (Coaching Sessions) and commitments to leverage new tools, frameworks, and approaches between coaching sessions. Your coach may also leverage assessment tools (e.g., personality inventories or peer feedback surveys), give homework assignments, and/or share books, articles, and videos for you to consider between meetings.

As professional coaches, we know that the best way to ensure a truly meaningful coaching experience is by 1) approaching the experience with a clear sense of what coaching is and how coaching can work for you, 2) launching the engagement with a genuine sense of trust and rapport, and 3) understanding and agreeing to a best-fit coaching process.

We also know how difficult this can be for people who have never worked with a coach, or perhaps would like to approach their next coaching experience with a higher standard for success. We wrote this book because we believe you should expect returns that greatly outweigh the costs of coaching. And where coaching experiences fall short of clients' expectations, it is usually for identifiable and preventable reasons.

Our intention in writing this book is simple: to help our clients understand all that coaching can be and how to approach the experience to get the most value possible.

How to Use This Book
The 2nd edition of *The Coaching Companion* is organized in a loosely chronological order, from start to finish of your coaching engagement. Section One is about setting yourself up for success; Section Two is about getting the most from each conversation, and Section Three is about persevering through coaching challenges. Each section

contains a number of helpful Tips. Each Tip includes an Application, which gives you a practical way to apply the tip with your coach, and a Tip in Action story—a real-life example of a client who put that particular tip into practice. These stories will help you to see both the context for the advice, and how others who may be facing similar challenges have applied each tip. In all cases, names have been changed to honor the confidentiality agreements that we have in place with these clients.

At the end of the book, you will find a Resources page which directs you to a website filled with tools and templates related to the Tips provided in this book. We sincerely hope that you'll leverage some of the resources we've designed for you.

The ideas presented in this book are relevant to all coaching experiences. They are not specific to any one type of person or coaching objective and will be useful to you regardless of your personal or professional development goals.

Whether you're getting ready for your first coaching experience or your next one, we hope that The Coaching Companion serves as a true companion—something you'll want to keep with you throughout the process to remind you, inspire you, and keep you on track toward getting all you can out of the coaching experience.

To your success,

Daniel and Carylynn

Section One:
Set Up for Success

Before you even enter into a coaching engagement, there are a number of things that you can do to be sure that you maximize your investment in coaching. Here we provide ten tips, which we view as essential building blocks for coaching:

Tip 1. Clarify Expectations
Tip 2. Cultivate Curiosity
Tip 3. Focus on What You Can Change
Tip 4. Leverage Feedback
Tip 5. Define Success
Tip 6. Visualize Success
Tip 7. Trust Your Coach
Tip 8. Create A Coaching Routine
Tip 9. Make a Personal Investment
Tip 10. Surround Yourself with Support

Tip 1. Clarify Expectations

"High achievement always takes place in the framework of high expectations."
– Charles Kettering

A mutual understanding of the respective expectations between you and your coach creates the foundation for a strong working relationship. Unclear and/or incongruent role expectations are a common cause of relational challenges.[1] Given that coaching is rooted in a trusting partnership between you and your coach, clarifying expectations is critical to successful engagement. In fact, all ICF-credentialed coaches are required to clarify expectations through a signed coaching contract. Ideally, contracts are discussed and signed during the first coaching session, and should include both your expectations for your coach as well as your coach's expectations of you.

Your Expectations for Your Coach

Starting out, you may not know what is reasonable or helpful to expect of your coach. Consider first your implicit expectations for others. For example, you may expect meetings to begin and end on time. Alternatively, you may expect your coach to be flexible with start and end times

---

[1] James Casanova et al., "Nurse-Physician Work Relations and Role Expectations," *JONA: The Journal of Nursing Administration* 37, no.2 (February 2007): 68-70.

given the unpredictability of your schedule. In order to ensure that your coach is best able to adapt to your style, such implicit expectations should be communicated explicitly, in conversation if not also in writing. Here are some additional factors to consider:

- What does confidentiality mean in the context of this coaching engagement?
- To what extent do you want your coach to challenge you?
- To what extent would you like your coach to help you think through a problem before offering advice?
- How much tangible support do you expect your coach to provide? What, in your mind, would this look like?

Your Coach's Expectations of You

Your coach's expectations of you are based on his or her experience and personal preferences. Some common examples of a coach's expectations of you may include:

- Being fully present during the coaching session.
- Being open and honest.
- Sending your agenda items in advance.
- If necessary, canceling sessions at least 48 hours in advance.
- Fulfilling homework obligations between coaching sessions.
- Willingness to speak to your coach if you aren't getting what you want from the coaching process.

If you have any questions or concerns about your coach's expectations of you, discuss them until all expectations are clarified before moving forward.

Emergent Expectations

Oftentimes, unmet expectations are actually emergent expectations—things that didn't come up in earlier conversations. For example, you might find yourself getting frustrated with your coach's questions when what you really want is advice. A conversation about any gaps between your expectations and what your coach is offering you can turn frustration and disappointment into insight and course corrections. Sometimes a simple and direct request made to your coach can get your coaching engagement back on track.

By proactively and continuously reflecting on and communicating your expectations to your coach, you increase the likelihood that your expectations will be met. In our experience, too many coaching relationships are only marginally effective—or fail altogether—because the coach and client have neglected to speak openly and candidly about their respective expectations.

Application

Periodically clarify, or perhaps revisit, expectations with your coach. Reference your Coaching Contract to see what expectations may be outlined there. Reflect on basic expectations that you hold for everyone in your life as well as your personal preference around timeliness, professionalism, directness, etc. Share your expectations with your coach and ask what you can expect from him or her.

Tip in Action

Lee, an associate director, was referred to a coach by his CEO. The CEO was concerned that Lee's direct approach upset members of senior management, and Lee set a goal to improve his interactions with them. Lee's coach laid out what Lee could expect from her: to share her observations for his consideration, to challenge his understanding of situations and of people, and to hold him accountable to commitments he made. This sounded reasonable, but Lee soon grew frustrated that his coach didn't entertain his venting nor sympathize with all of his frustrations.

Fortunately, Lee's coach sensed that Lee needed to vent and made a proposal: Lee could vent all he wished for the first 5 minutes of each coaching session, but after that time was up, he had to stop venting and start exploring ways to manage his frustrations. Lee enthusiastically agreed. After all, he didn't actually want to spend the entire coaching session just venting.

In this case, Lee's coach initiated the shift in expectations. Perhaps next time they need to tweak their expectations, the suggestion will come from Lee.

Tip 2. Cultivate Curiosity

"Change how you look at things and the things you look at will change."
—Wayne Dyer

Curiosity, the intrinsic motivation to learn, is an important quality to adopt from the start of your coaching experience. Research shows that curiosity increases our propensity to explore, learn through challenges, and question our beliefs and assumptions.[2] This same set of activities is foundational to coaching. In other words, curiosity is the foundation on which coaching is built. The good news is that you were born curious.[3] The bad news is that, as an adult learner, you will now have to work hard to embrace the sense of wonder that makes children such sponges for new skills and information. Think about it: have you ever met an adult who didn't have self-limiting beliefs? By cultivating curiosity, you can begin to see where your beliefs support and limit your growth.

---

[2] Kimberly S. Ladd, "The Experiences of Students Who Increased Curiosity During Their First Year of College: A Grounded Theory Study," *Dissertation Abstracts International Section A: Humanities and Social Sciences* 80, (2019): 3-A(E).

[3] Dajung Diane Shin and Sun-il Kim, "Homo Curious: Curious or Interested?" *Educational Psychological Review* 31, no.4 (December 2019): 853-74, http://doi.org/10.1007/s10648-019-09497-x.

Moving Beyond *I Know*

Curiosity is the antidote to getting stuck in the *I know* mindset. Curiosity prevents you from jumping to conclusions and helps you to recognize and question assumptions and deeply-held beliefs. Assuming complete knowledge of anything can be a tremendous barrier to personal growth. For example, if you *know* what good communication looks like, you're probably not very interested in learning new methods and techniques for effective communication. Similarly, you are far more likely to try your hand at something if you are curious whether you can do it, rather than *knowing* that you can or can't do it. Curiosity creates new possibilities by moving you beyond *I know*.

Strengthening Curiosity

KnowInnovation, an organization that engages top scientists in "deliberate creativity" to solve the world's most complex problems, encourages us to treat curiosity like a switch that you can turn on. By visualizing a curiosity switch in your brain, you can choose to activate curiosity. And while the neurology of curiosity is still far from mapped out or understood, it is our experience that the more you exercise curiosity in new and different ways, the easier it becomes to do so. In addition to turning on that curiosity switch of imagination, you can build your capacity to be curious by:

- Consulting others, even when you don't think you need to.
- Asking, *what else* and *why* multiple times over.
- Asking lots of follow-up questions.

- Adopt a beginner's mindset. Assume that you don't know much, even in an area in which you think you're an expert.

It is never too early or too late to begin exercising your curiosity pathways! Simply put, your coach can't teach you anything that you don't want to learn.

Application

Notice your use of absolute language (e.g., "That will never work"). Practice transforming absolute statements into less absolute terms, for example, by beginning the statements with the phrase, "It seems…" (e.g., "It seems that will never work").

For one week, have at least one conversation per day in which you practice extreme curiosity. As you listen to others, think of at least one follow-up question you might ask, even if you think you know what the answer might be. Alternatively, if you catch yourself adhering too rigidly to an assumption, think of a way to challenge that assumption. Leverage curiosity to probe your *I know* mindset.

Tip in Action

Don began working with a coach when he realized that he did not want to become a part of his current company's senior leadership team. Don felt disconnected with the company's values and wanted to explore opportunities outside the company.

Don entered the coaching relationship *knowing* that his career path was somewhere within his current industry. He had worked in the industry for thirty years. Don didn't see any future for himself outside it—not for lack of interest but simply because he *knew* that no other company would be interested in him. Don's coach challenged him to reflect on how well this assumption served him. Don agreed to question his belief, and in doing so, he realized that his leadership skills were transferable to positions in many sectors. Don discovered many unexpected opportunities, and he realized that these opportunities only presented themselves after he declared himself a beginner in the domain of his own job search.

Tip 3. Focus on What You Can Change

"You have power over your mind—not outside events. Realize this, and you will find strength."
– Marcus Aurelius

One of the first things that your coach will explore with you is your goals. As you consider the various things that you could discuss with your coach, it's critical to focus your efforts on those things that you can change.

Identifying Your Circle of Influence
In his life-changing work on *The 7 Habits of Highly Effective People*, Stephen Covey reminds us that there's a critical distinction between our Circle of Concern and our Circle of Influence. Your Circle of Concern contains things that you care about but have little control over—others' attitudes, behavior, and responses to change, for example. By contrast, your Circle of Influence contains the things that you have the greatest influence over—your behavior, attitudes, and even beliefs. As you consider the things that you could discuss with your coach, remember that coaching focuses squarely on your ability to grow and to have greater impact. As a result, your coaching goals should focus on items that are within your Circle of Influence—the inner circle. For example, let's say that you're concerned about the motivation of Joe, a member of your team. Joe's motivation is within your Circle of Concern, but not your Circle of Influence, as you simply

cannot change other people. What does lie within your Circle of Influence is the way that you communicate with Joe, which may in fact influence his motivation. To focus on what you can change, make sure that your coaching goals address items within your Circle of Influence, not just your Circle of Concern.

THE CIRCLE OF INFLUENCE

Source: Stephen Covey, The 7 Habits of Highly Effective People   Design by Kanza Enriquez / © Creating Open Space LLC

Diving Beneath the Surface

As you consider what's within your Circle of Control, consider not only the behaviors you'd like to change (e.g., how you manage conflict or how you boost your team's performance), but also the underlying thoughts and feelings (e.g., assumptions, beliefs, and expectations) that drive your approach. In fact, we strongly recommend that you *start* with shifts in what and how you think and feel. When you start by shifting your thoughts and feelings, shifts in your behavior have integrity. By contrast, when you try to shift your behavior without first shifting your thoughts and feelings, you run the risk of coming across as fake.

THE ICEBURG MODEL

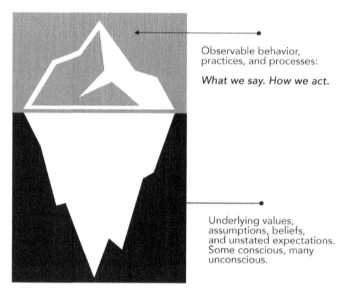

Observable behavior, practices, and processes:

What we say. How we act.

Underlying values, assumptions, beliefs, and unstated expectations. Some conscious, many unconscious.

Sonja Sackmann: Uncovering Culture in Organizations   Design by Kariza Enriquez / © Creating Open Space LLC

To begin this journey into the deep (sometimes dark) recesses of your mind, start at a specific point on the surface. For example, choose a specific relationship that you'd like to improve, then identify one specific thing you'd like to do differently when you're talking with this person. Dive in from here: to make this change, what would you need to think? What would you need to feel? What assumptions would you need to set aside? Enlist your coach to help you in this process.

Application

Draw your Circle of Concern, and within that, your Circle of Influence. In your Circle of Concern, list all the things that you would like to be different. In your Circle of Influence, list the things that you have control over, including your thoughts and feelings, which you could leverage to influence the items in your Circle of Concern.

Tip in Action

Lily, Beau and Tom had all grown frustrated with their boss, who made them feel like robots paid to execute his plans. Each engaged a coach with the goal of improving their ability to work with this difficult leader, yet each went about it differently.

Despite his coach's efforts to help him focus on what he could change, Tom's attention was consumed by all the things that Tom wanted his boss to do differently. At best, Tom half-heartedly agreed to try a few different tactics with his boss, but they didn't really help, and Tom's boss didn't magically change in the ways that Tom wished he would.

Beau realized from the start that he couldn't change his boss, and eagerly sought out different ways to engage. For example, in an effort to get his point across, Beau tried asking more questions, but his questions came across as critical and judgmental, and his boss didn't respond well.

Like Beau, Lily realized that she couldn't change her boss, and focused on what she could change. But Lily didn't feel comfortable trying different tactics—she wanted to feel differently about her boss. As a result, Lily first sought out a deeper appreciation for her boss's approach. First she identified assumptions she was making, for example, that he didn't care what she thought, and put them to the side. Then she listened and asked questions from a place of genuine curiosity. Not surprisingly, the boss responded much more positively to Lily's questions than to Beau's questions. Over time, he began opening up and explaining his thinking and rationale to her. Once Lily understood his goals and concerns, she was able to adjust her recommendations and approach accordingly. By focusing first on her thoughts and feelings—including faulty assumptions and beliefs—Lily was about to shift her approach in an authentic way. As is often the case, Lily's approach of changing her feelings was far more effective than Beau's approach (adjusting his approach without adjusting his thoughts/feelings) or Tom's approach (wishing the boss would change).

Tip 4. Leverage Feedback

"Negative feedback can make us bitter or better."
— Robin Sharma

As you refine your focus area(s) into coaching goals, it's important to guard against blind spots. Joseph Luft and Harrington Ingham's classic Johari Window defines blind spots as behaviors or characteristics that are known to others but not to oneself.

THE JOHARI WINDOW

	INCOMPETENT	COMPETENT
CONSCIOUS	**Consciously Incompetent** ▪▪▪ *"I know that I don't know"*	**Consciously Competent** ▪▪▪ *"I know that I know"*
UNCONSCIOUS	**Unconsciously Incompetent** ▪▪▪ *"I don't know that I don't know"*	**Unconsciously Competent** ▪▪▪ *"I don't know that I know"*

Feedback and assessment tools are exceptionally helpful for revealing blind spots. Even if you feel that your boss, colleagues, team members, clients and stakeholders are all perfectly candid with you (which is rarely the case), your coach will likely want to gather feedback in a more direct and structured way. Gathering feedback through your coach has a couple of benefits:

- Your coach can design a way for feedback to be provided anonymously, which maximizes candor.
- When a coach is able to receive feedback directly, he or she knows that the feedback is unfiltered—e.g., it's someone's authentic perception of you, not your perception of their perception of you.

Forms of Feedback

Feedback comes in many forms. Common feedback strategies often include performance reviews, customer feedback surveys, engagement surveys, and measures of physical health. Most of our coaching clients want more in-depth feedback than they've already received. As such, we often leverage formal 360-degree feedback tools, in which you select anywhere from about 5 to 15 people to collect feedback from, and compare feedback across groups (e.g., your boss(es), peers, direct reports, and other stakeholders). In addition or as an alternative to 360 surveys, many coaches prefer to gather qualitative information by interviewing a handful of people whose feedback you value. When we do these interviews, we like to co-create the questions we ask with our clients.

It's important to be open to a variety of forms of feedback. Any given piece of feedback is simply a data point. It doesn't define you—it simply tells you something about how others see you.

Receiving Feedback

Let's face it. Receiving feedback can feel absolutely gut-wrenching, even when the people who offer it have the best intentions and highest aspirations for us. More often than not, feedback creates a fight, flight, or freeze response. These emotional reactions literally shut down our ability to think rationally, making it hard to hear, much less consider, the information being offered to us. Furthermore, our brains focus on the negative comments more than the positive, so feedback that was intended for good can often result in discouragement, defensiveness, and disengagement. To make feedback work for you instead of against you, you'll have to move through these emotions. On the other side of your emotional reaction is a place where you're ready and willing to receive feedback and do something with it. Our three favorite approaches to calm emotional reactions to feedback include Grounding, Reframing, and Empathizing.

Grounding

Grounding is a technique that reduces emotional reactions by bringing attention to your physical surroundings. In today's workplace, the physical environment is typically safe. The air is safe to breathe, the floor is sturdy beneath your feet. Bringing attention to your breath, for example, reminds you that you are alive and well—the threat is all in your head. Breathing in a slow consistent way brings stability to your heart rate, which further signals your brain that all is well and promotes clarity of thought. This is the wisdom of the saying, *just breathe.*

Reframing

Reframing is a way to take a thought that makes us emotional and transform it into a thought that makes us think. For example, a client of mine recently got some feedback from his boss. The boss felt that he was micromanaging his team. My client's initial thought was, *"What right does he have to say this when he does the same thing to me?"* That thought was filled with a sense of unfairness, which was triggering a strong negative reaction. To reframe his response, he decided to think, *"It's good to know that he dislikes micromanagement, and we both have blind spots."* Notice that his new framing was much more empowering—rather than discounting the feedback as unfair, it gave him something to work on.

Empathizing

Finally, even if you don't agree with the feedback, and even if you don't appreciate the way that the feedback was delivered, you can still appreciate the person who took the risk to give it to you. To do so, activate empathy for the person giving you the feedback: remind yourself of how difficult it can be to give feedback, and remember how it feels to be really uncomfortable. The number one reason that people don't give tough feedback is because they're concerned about how people will respond. Showing that you sincerely appreciate their willingness to be uncomfortable is a sure way to get more feedback from colleagues in the future.

Application

Ask your coach to recommend one or more assessments and to review the results with you. Consider selecting assessments that reflect different aspects of being (e.g., personality, leadership, emotional intelligence, conflict management style). Be willing to discuss both the results that confirm your beliefs about yourself and those that do not.

Tip in Action

Lisa was deeply disturbed by her leadership assessment report. "Have you ever seen anyone with scores so bad?" she asked her coach. "Should I just quit?" Lisa's coach encouraged her to breathe through these initial emotional reactions, then think more deeply about what insights the feedback, on the whole, might offer her.

As Lisa explored the patterns in the data, such as an indicator that she was too passive in senior management meetings, her eyes opened to a new possibility. Could it be that her scores reflected the potential that people saw in her? Lisa explored a new story. Her people believed in her; they wanted her to rise into even greater positions of leadership, and they wanted to help prepare her for the demands of that next level. Lisa bravely shared this new interpretation with a few trusted colleagues. They validated that while Lisa would need to be more assertive and more decisive at the next level of leadership, they genuinely wanted to see her rise through the ranks and were confident that she would rise to such challenges as they presented themselves.

Tip 5. Define Success

"It's not about wealth and fame and power. It's about how many shining eyes
I have around me."
— Benjamin Zander's definition of success

At this point you're ready to define success for your coaching engagement. In the context of coaching, success is typically defined as the accomplishment of a specific set of coaching goals. Coaching goals may include *growth goals* (e.g., things that you would like to be able to do differently) and *outcome goals* (e.g., success on a certain project, successful transition into a new role, strengthened team dynamics, or even a promotion).

The Impact of Setting Goals

It's well documented that writing down your goals, in particular goals that are important to you and energize you, increases the likelihood that you will accomplish them. In his extensive research on wealthy entrepreneurs, Thomas Corley found that setting and then pursuing goals was one of the distinguishing characteristics of self-made millionaires.[4] Goals help you focus on what's really important, prioritize limited resources, measure progress, and hold yourself accountable. The act of writing down

---

[4] Tom Corley, *Change Your Habits, Change Your Life: Strategies that Transformed 177 Average People into Self-Made Millionaires* (Minneapolis: North Loop Books, 2016).

your goals helps you gain clarity about what's really important to you.

Goal Hierarchies

Importantly, goals are nested into goal hierarchies, simply meaning that a high-level (aka, *superordinate*) goal can be broken down into a number of supporting (aka, *subordinate*) goals.[5] Both kinds of goals are relevant to coaching. In many cases, a high-level goal frames an entire coaching engagement. For example, it may take an entire coaching engagement to rebuild trust with a business partner. This high-level goal will create the context for exploring numerous supporting goals, which may include improved listening, building empathy, and being more direct. In your initial conversations with your coach, it's helpful to define both high-level and supporting goals.

EXAMPLES OF COACHING GOALS

HIGH-LEVEL 'Superordinate'	SUPPORTING 'Subordinate'
Strengthening trust	✓ Improved listening ✓ Greater empathy ✓ More directness ✓ Greater self-confidence
Influencing up	✓ Stronger negotiation skills ✓ Broader perspective-taking ✓ Political savvy

---

[5] David M. Bridgeland and Ron Zahavi, *Business Modeling: A Practical Guide to Realizing Business Value* (Burlington: Morgan Kaufmann Publishers, 2018).

What About Competing Goals?

All too often, our high-level goals appear to compete with one another, as if the accomplishment of one translates to a failure to achieve the other. For example, if you aspire to put family first, that may appear to compete with your goal of getting promoted to a Senior VP level in your organization. When you find yourself pursuing competing goals, it's important to question the assumption that they can't coexist. Many times, things we see as either/or dilemmas can be translated into both/and opportunities. Bring these dilemmas to your coach, and be ready to explore how you might, indeed, have it both ways.

One vs. Many Goals

Beware of the tendency to pursue more than one high-level goal at a given time. It is necessary to explore multiple supporting goals when you are working toward achieving a high-level goal, but focusing on even two or three high-level goals often results in moderate progress at best.[6] Moderate progress rarely produces the shift you hope to see, and therefore generates little motivation. By comparison, when you focus intently on only one big goal, you are more likely to make remarkable, notable progress in that area. When you make a real shift—even if in only one area—others notice, and the acknowledgement you receive will create momentum that helps to fuel the pursuit of your next high-level goal.

---

[6] Amy Dalton and Stephen Spiller, "Too Much of a Good Thing: The Benefits of Implementation Intentions Depend on the Number of Goals," *Journal of Consumer Research* 39, no.3 (October 2012): 600-14.

Getting Started

Given that supporting goals often emerge through coaching conversations, focus first on clarifying your high-level goals. If your goal is so high-level that it cannot be accomplished within your current coaching engagement, identify a milestone for which you want to be able to celebrate success in your last meeting with your coach. With this level of goal in mind, leverage the acronym SMART: make your goal Specific, Measurable, Actionable, Realistic, and Time-bound. Take your goal-setting one step further and write out what and how things will be different—for you and for others—when this goal is accomplished.

Application

If possible, identify a high-level goal for your coaching engagement and clarify it using the SMART paradigm. Then, write a paragraph or two about what and how things will be different when this goal is accomplished. Share this with your coach.

If you have a difficult time identifying a high-level goal for your coaching engagement, share this reality with your coach. Engage your coach in a conversation that is centered on clarifying your goals.

Tip in Action

Harold was provided with a coach as a part of his leadership development program. When asked what he wanted to get out of coaching, his first response was a genuine, *"I don't know."* Harold said those words apologetically, as if he had already failed at coaching in some way. But Harold's coach was not surprised—it's not uncommon for people to need help thinking through their coaching goals.

Fortunately, Harold didn't get stuck on *"I don't know."* He patiently worked through the follow-up questions his coach asked—questions like, *"What are the things that are most important to you?"*, *"If you could impact one thing before leaving this earth, what would that be?"* and *"If there's one superpower you could have, what would that be and what would it do for you?"*. Somewhere along the way, Harold realized that while everything was going well for him, he also had a passion for racial equality that he had never been able to integrate into his work. As soon as he surfaced this passion, it was like an itch that simply had to be scratched. At that moment, Harold's high-level coaching goal emerged: *"To activate my passion for racial equality in my leadership by using my voice and my talents to significantly increase racial diversity at the top of the company."* This goal became a star that Harold deeply wanted to reach, and from it, many supporting goals quickly emerged—like how to talk about racial justice in a non-threatening way.

Tip 6. Visualize Success

"Man can only see what he sees himself receiving."
— Florence Scovel Shinn

Once you have defined success, you're ready to employ the power of visualization. Visualization has repeatedly been proven as a great accelerator of success. For example:

- The men's gymnastics team at Stanford found that visualization of complex performance elements helped them to increase their flexibility and eliminate timing errors.[7]
- Natan Sharansky beat a world champion chess player after 10 years of visualizing chess games while in solitary confinement.[8]
- Jack Nicklaus, Michael Jordan, and Muhammad Ali each attributed their success to their consistent use of visualization—each swing, each shot, each punch.[9]

As these examples demonstrate, visualization works when you visualize *the process* of accomplishing that goal.

---

[7] Matt Mayberry, "The Extraordinary Power of Visualizing Your Success," *Business Insider,* February 14, 2015, http://www.businessinsider.com/the-extraordinary-power-of-visualizing-your-success-2015-2.

[8] Srinivasan Pillay, "The Science of Visualization: Maximizing Your Brain's Potential During The Recession," *HuffPost*, November 17, 2011, http://www.huffpost.com/static/about-us.

[9] Matthew Toren, "If You Envision It, It Will Come," *Entrepreneur*, April 6, 2014, http://www.entrepreneur.com/article/232813.

How Visualization Works

Visualization is believed to influence our success in a few nuanced ways. For one, when you visualize yourself working toward and accomplishing a goal—each action, each effort, each successive setback and success—your brain actually activates many of the same neural pathways that will be activated when you actually take these actions.[10] Let's say for example, that you would like to be more effective at initiating difficult conversations. By visualizing yourself approaching a person you need to talk to, bringing up the difficult topic, managing your tone, body language, and emotions, and ultimately being satisfied with the outcome, you are literally giving yourself the gift of practice. Thus, when it's time to have a difficult conversation, your body already has neural pathways built to support your success.

Visualization also works by creating completely new memories, which prime our brain to notice the things that align with goal accomplishment.[11,12] Specifically,

---

[10] Jim Lohr, "Can Visualizing Your Body Doing Something Help You Learn To Do It Better?" Scientific American, May 1, 2015, http://www.scientificamerican.com/article/can-visualizing-your-body-doing-something-help-you-learn-to-do-it-better/.

[11] Daniel L. Schacter et al., "The Future of Memory: Remembering, Imagining, and the Brain," *PubMed Central*, (November 2013): http://www.ncbi.nlm.nih.gov/pmc/articles/PMC3815616/.

[12] "The Reticular Activating System and Visualization," The Higher Path Project, http://thehigherpathproject.com/visualization-reticular-activating-system/.

visualization activates the occipital lobe,[13] the part of the subconscious brain that scans the environment for stimuli, filters out all the noise, and selects what we should bring into conscious awareness. When you visualize yourself accomplishing a goal, you are literally increasing the amount of brainpower you're dedicating to pursuing that goal.[14]

Visualization Strategies

Although we all inherently know how to visualize, there are several strategies that increase the impact of visualization.

- **Move from third person to first person.** Most people first visualize themselves in the third person—as if they are having an out of body experience, seeing themselves in action. Visualizing in the third person helps you to step back and look at the bigger picture. Most of the time, it's also helpful to move from third person to first person visualization, as if you are in your own body, seeing things through your own eyes. Visualizing in the first person is more likely to evoke emotions, which makes first person visualization more likely to activate the subconscious mechanisms discussed above. An exception to this rule is when first person visualization is too emotional—when visualizing yourself engaging in a situation is so

---

[13] Christopher Taibbi, "Brain Basics, Part One: The Power of Visualization," *Psychology Today*, November 4, 2012, http://www.psychologytoday.com/us/blog/gifted-ed-guru/201211/brain-basics-part-one-the-power-visualization.

[14] "Understand Your Brain to Use Visualization," John Assaraf, Accessed October 31, 2020, http://johnassaraf.com/understand-your-brain-to-use-visualization/.

stressful or otherwise threatening that you can't see yourself through to success.

- **Use all of your senses.** Contrary to its label, visualization includes seeing, hearing, smelling, tasting and touching. An image may first come to mind, but before following that image into action, pause and visualize what you hear, what you smell, what you taste, and even what you're touching. For example, to fully visualize a difficult conversation, you would want to hear the background noises, smell and taste the coffee in your mug, feel the chair you're sitting in, and notice the tightness in your shoulders, the dryness in your mouth and the temperature in the room. Notice that to fully use all of your senses, you will have to shift from third to first person visualization.

- **Include emotions.** Have you ever noticed that almost all of your memories are tied to emotion? We remember moments of great joy, surprise, and disappointment, and quickly forget nearly everything in between. By extension, in order for a visualization to be solidified to long-term memory, it must include emotional highs and/or lows. If you're visualizing a difficult conversation, you might tune into your fear and anxiety, your determination, and your sense of relief after the conversation is over.

Application

Visualize yourself accomplishing a goal that you've set for your coaching engagement. After visualizing what it will look and feel like to be successful, move backwards from that moment until today. Visualize the conversations you will need to have. Visualize both the support and resistance likely to come from others. Visualize actions and conversations that are difficult for you and visualize yourself managing the discomfort of an encounter you would rather avoid.

Tip in Action

Isaiah knew that he wanted to rise through the ranks to become a senior leader. He loved many aspects of leadership, from driving results to helping others grow and succeed. When Isaiah first began to work with his coach, his vision was clear but lacking detail and context: he saw himself at the top, reporting only to the Board, working with and through his senior leadership team. The trouble was, Isaiah's vision wasn't working for him. He had been stuck in the same Director-level role for 5 years now, and no one was talking to him about a promotion.

Isaiah's coach challenged him to fill in the gaps between *now* and *then* in his vision, and also to begin to visualize the way he would lead at each level in between. Soon, Isaiah had a clear vision of how he would lead as a Senior Director, as an Associate Vice President, a Vice President, and a Senior Vice President. He also began to visualize his accomplishments at each level—things so noteworthy they would make him stand out for promotion. Isaiah was wise not to limit his vision to tactical wins like growth in market share. Rather, he also envisioned how he would grow market share—by empowering his people to discover and use their strengths, increasing diversity, and strengthening collaboration. Most importantly, however, Isaiah's vision grew to include how he could begin to do these things right now, at his current level. Isaiah's ability to maximize his team's strengths, increase diversity, and strengthen collaboration within his organization did indeed get noticed. Within a year he received his first promotion, and he shows no sign of slowing down.

Tip 7. Trust Your Coach

"Trust is the glue of life."
— Stephen R. Covey

It is absolutely essential that you trust your coach enough to have authentic conversations and interactions. This is not to say that you need to trust your coach for absolutely everything. You certainly wouldn't trust your coach to do open heart surgery. Likewise, unless you hired a coach to tell you what to do, you don't necessarily need to trust that your coach could do your job for you. What should you be able to trust your coach to do during your engagement sessions?

The Foundation for Trust

In *Working at the Speed of Trust*, Stephen R. Covey defines four Cores of Credibility that serve as the foundation for trust in relationships: Integrity, Intent, Capabilities, and Results. Through this lens, it is essential that you trust that your coach:

- Works with the utmost integrity, for example, that he or she will maintain any confidentiality agreement that you have discussed.
- Has good intentions, for example, that his or her agenda is your agenda, within the bounds of the coaching engagement.
- Is successful as a coach. In other words, that he or she can do their job well.

Individual Differences

It is helpful to realize that the act of extending trust is more difficult for some than others. Some people trust instinctively, unless and until that trust is betrayed. Others tend to reserve trust for those who prove themselves trustworthy. Identifying where you lie on this spectrum of extending trust can help you understand how to build and retain trust with your coach.

INDIVIDUAL DIFFERENCES IN TRUST

	IF YOU TEND TO...	
	INSTINCTIVELY TRUST	INSTINCTIVELY DISTRUST
IT CAN HELP TO...	✓ Proactively communicate your expectations, and ask if your coach can meet them. ✓ Don't take confidentiality for granted; explore its guarantee and any exceptions in the context of your coaching engagement.	✓ Ask questions to accelerate your vetting process. ✓ Take minor risks by sharing things that give your coach a chance to be trustworthy. ✓ Watch out for biases; almost all of us distrust some group of people as a result of our life experiences.

Implications of Distrust

An ounce of distrust is like poison to a coaching relationship, because even a hint of distrust will shut down your ability to think clearly and expansively. That said, it is one thing to give your coach time to prove him or herself, and quite another to continue a coaching relationship after you have decided that your coach doesn't deserve your trust. Before you decide on the latter, try to share your concerns with your coach. In many cases, distrust is a result of communication gaps rather than a lack of Integrity, Intent, Capabilities, or Results. Your coach, like yourself, is human, and therefore humanly imperfect. Most coaches dedicate their lives to learning alongside their clients, and respond quite well to feedback. If you're at a loss for words, you might start with something like this: *"I've been reading about how trust is absolutely essential for coaching. For this (coaching) to be worth our time, I have to feel comfortable sharing openly and honestly. Unfortunately, as things stand, I don't feel that way."* Sometimes such conversations reveal breakthroughs. Sometimes, they only solidify your doubts. If you ask good questions but don't respect the answers, take risks to share personally but don't appreciate your coach's response, and/or have a conversation about your discomfort that doesn't make you feel better, it's probably time to find a new coach.

Application

Reflect on how you form trusting relationships with others, considering both your professional and personal relationships. Share any insights you gain from this reflection activity with your coach. Also share any reservations you have regarding being completely open and honest with your coach.

Tip in Action

Lucy is an inherently trusting person. She naturally gives people the benefit of the doubt and believes that with rare exceptions, people have good intentions even when they make mistakes. Lucy trusted her coach because she had no reason not to, so it never occurred to ask her coach if he or she was coaching anyone else in her organization.

A few months went by before Lucy discovered her coach was also working with a colleague from another division—not just any colleague, but the person with whom Lucy had the most difficulty. Lucy's trust in her coach was threatened by this revelation. She feared that her coach would not be able to coach them both without revealing the privileged content of their discussions to each other.

If Lucy had let this fear manifest as a lack of trust in her coach's ability to maintain confidentiality, she could have lost the ability to address issues she had with this coworker. Instead Lucy shared her concern with her coach. The coach listened, empathized with Lucy's concern, reiterated their confidentiality agreement, and shared a few examples of how the coach had navigated similar situations in the past. Lucy's coach also provided a few hypothetical examples of how he might leverage his understanding of this difficult colleague to inform his coaching approach. As a result of this initially uncomfortable conversation, Lucy felt relieved and more confident in her coach than ever.

Tip 8. Create A Coaching Routine

"Things that matter most must never be at the mercy of things which matter least."
– Goethe

Coaching is a bit like exercise: it's the routine, not any given workout, that will propel you to accomplish your goals. As such, creating a reliable coaching routine is absolutely essential. Coaching routines generally come in two forms: coaching sessions, and exercises between coaching sessions.

Coaching Sessions

Coaching sessions are much like personal training sessions. These tend to be high-intensity workouts in which your coach introduces you to new and sometimes painful exercises, all for the purpose of helping you reach your goals. If your coaching sessions are scheduled inconsistently or arbitrarily, it will be difficult for each coaching session to build on the last one. In a sense, it may feel that you're starting from scratch with each session. To set yourself up for success, design a cadence of coaching sessions that makes sense given your goals and the timeframes surrounding those goals. For example, you may want to see quick results, along with support for making the changes last. In this case, it could make sense to meet weekly for a month or two, and then monthly thereafter. Alternatively, you may want support through a job transition, in which case it could make sense to meet once every two to three weeks. In situations in which you're struggling to manage daily challenges, it may help to meet weekly until you feel more confident that you have things under control.

Exercises Between Sessions

A strong coaching routine will include exercises between sessions. It isn't necessary, nor advisable for that matter, to pre-determine such exercises. The best exercises are those that build on the muscles you've strengthened during a coaching session to prepare you for the next coaching session. Ideally, you can co-create such exercises with your coach. At times, however, your coach will ask you to engage in an exercise that you may not understand or even see the value in. This is a great opportunity to trust your coach, which is an opportunity for growth in itself.

Easy to Say, Hard to Do

Coaches realize that it is incredibly difficult to be consistent with coaching sessions and exercises. For many, a coaching session feels like one more thing to fit into a lengthy list of responsibilities. Even when you find the time, your coaching sessions and activities can easily be displaced by unpredictable events. Here are a few specific tips on how to establish and proactively protect your coaching routine:

- Strategically choose a day and time for your coaching sessions—one that is least likely to be interrupted by unplanned meetings and events. In this way, your session can serve as an anchor to your otherwise hectic schedule.

- If you have someone who manages your calendar, let them know that your coaching session is a top priority.
- Delegate additional responsibilities to free up time to engage more fully in your coaching exercises.
- Consider saying no to new commitments—at least for now. Note: If you're the type of person who frequently finds yourself overcommitted, this will be especially important.

Application

Reflect and/or journal on the following questions:

- How can my coaching engagements be scheduled so that they offer me something predictable, and even something that I can look forward to?
- What can I do today to set expectations for my availability among my clients, colleagues, and even friends and family?

Tip in Action

William, a transportation-planning executive, had grown accustomed to rescheduling appointments due to competing priorities. When he began preparing for his first coaching engagement, he decided to do what he could to change the expectations of his colleagues of his availability, as he was dedicated to getting the most he could out of the process. Lacking a way to express this, he worked with his coach prior to their first meeting to develop a short script he could use to ensure that the time he would dedicate to coaching would be protected. William then shared with his team: *"Just so you know, I'm going to be busier than usual in the coming months. I'm going to be working with a coach to develop my leadership skills. We will be meeting on Thursday afternoons from 4:00 to 5:30 for the next twelve weeks. This time is important to me. I'd like your help running defense on any meetings or responsibilities that could impact my ability to make these appointments."*

Tip 9. Make a Personal Investment

"For where your treasure is, there your heart will be also."
– Matthew 21:6 (Holy Bible, New International Version)

Like many things in life, the results you get out of coaching will be proportional to the work that you put into it. In our experience, those who pay for coaching out of pocket are the most engaged, most proactive, and least likely to waste a moment in a coaching session. But for many individuals, the cost of coaching is prohibitive. Organizations, on the other hand, view the cost of coaching as pennies to the dollar compared to the exorbitant costs of unnecessary turnover and/or poor leadership. If you are the recipient of pro-bono coaching or coaching that is paid for by your employer, this tip is particularly relevant to you. It is important to invest a high level of engagement in the coaching process, even if the monetary cost isn't your responsibility.

The Psychology of Consumption

Research has pointed to several patterns between cost and consumption. These include:

- The cost of a product or service has a profound impact on the likelihood that it will be consumed; products and services that we pay for are much more likely to be consumed than those offered to us for free.

- When products and services are paid for by a third party (for example, an employer), awareness of the cost paid boosts consumption.
- The timing of payment impacts consumption—we are much more likely to consume something that we paid for recently than something we paid for a long time ago.[15]

All of these patterns play out in the realm of coaching services. At one extreme, free coaching is often left on the table: clients are less likely to prioritize meetings, less likely to prepare for meetings, and less likely to follow through on coaching conversations. At the other extreme, clients who are paying for coaching out of pocket almost universally prioritize, prepare for, and follow through on meetings. Clients who know how much their organization has invested in their coaching engagement typically fall somewhere in the middle. These psychological mechanisms are quite strong and pervasive, and should serve as a warning for those who are fortunate enough to receive coaching without paying out of pocket: beware of depreciating the value of things that are given to you.

Ways to Personally Invest in Coaching

To appreciate the value of a gift, you must begin to invest in the gift itself. In the context of coaching, the most obvious way that people do this is with their time. At the very least, you will need to dedicate precious time to preparing for any given coaching session, to meeting with

---

[15] John T. Gourville and Dilip Soman, "Pricing and the Psychology of Consumption," *Harvard Business Review*, (September 2002): http://hbr.org/2002/09/pricing-and-the-psychology-of-consumption.

your coach, and to doing your homework in between sessions (see also Tip 8). You may also incur some personal expenses along the way—a meal that you can't charge to the corporate card, a parking fee, or an extra resource that your coach recommends to you. These are very basic ways to personally invest in your coaching engagement but they are unlikely to provide enough motivation for you. To leverage the psychology of consumption in your favor, you will have to contribute to your coaching engagement in a way that makes anything less than 110% effort feel wasteful. Here are some ways to meaningfully invest yourself in coaching, starting small and going big:

- When you meet your coach for coffee or lunch, cover the bill.
- Use personal time off to prepare for a coaching session or to meet with your coach.
- Invest in a weekend retreat where everything is set up to promote self-reflection and deep work.
- Deepen your coaching experience by purchasing resources that weren't covered by your employer, such as an interview-based 360.
- Pay for someone who does not have the financial resources for coaching (e.g., the head of a local non-profit, an emerging leader in your community) to work with a coach.
- Donate the cost of your coaching engagement (or the personal financial value of accomplishing your coaching objectives) to a cause that you would not have otherwise given to.

Application

Using the formula below, identify the gap between (A) the value of your coaching engagement, and (B) your current level of personal investment.

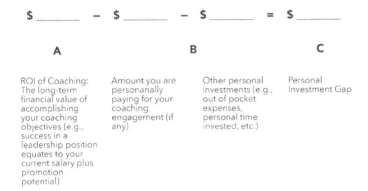

$ _____ \quad - \quad $ _____ \quad - \quad $ _____ \quad = \quad $ _____

A	B		C
ROI of Coaching: The long-term financial value of accomplishing your coaching objectives (e.g., success in a leadership position equates to your current salary plus promotion potential)	Amount you are personanally paying for your coaching engagement (if any)	Other personal investments (e.g., out of pocket expenses, personal time invested, etc.)	Personal Investment Gap

After this Personal Investment Gap (C) is identified, make a list of ways that you can close it such that you are investing at least—if not more—in your coaching than your employer and/or your coach.

Tip in Action

Jemal, a Program Director at a large organization, was incredibly grateful that his boss granted his request for leadership and career coaching. If he could only get to that next level—a true leadership position—many more career opportunities would be open to him. Without being prompted to do so, Jemal began to personally invest in his coaching engagement. First, he began taking every other Friday off so that he could clear his mind and focus on himself. He purposefully scheduled his coaching sessions on these biweekly days off, which had the added benefit of buffering him from interruptions. Whenever possible, Jemal scheduled his coaching session over morning coffee or lunch, and insisted on paying the entire bill. Jemal also covered the cost of several additional items out of pocket, including a strengths assessment and a personality profile.

About mid-way through his coaching engagement, Jemal realized that many of his peers could benefit from coaching too. He took it upon himself to advocate for the expansion of coaching to all who requested it, and did the legwork to get a coaching contract in place. All of these personal investments strengthened Jemal's commitment to the coaching process. He faithfully came prepared to meetings, worked through challenging insights, and did his homework.

Tip 10. Surround Yourself with Support

"You are not alone."
— Alcoholics Anonymous mantra

Your beliefs and behaviors are heavily influenced by the people around you.[16] Peer influence doesn't end in adulthood, nor is it limited to the classic examples of smoking and drinking. Whether you realize it or not, the people you spend time with will either support or hinder your progress of growth and transformation. Think of the last time you wanted to invest in yourself, perhaps by enrolling in a class or pursuing a career shift: who encouraged you, and how did that impact you? On the flip side, who was skeptical or negative, and what impact did this have on you? Whenever you are pursuing personal growth, you need all the energy you can get to face challenges and secure new opportunities. In order to make the changes you seek, you need to surround yourself with people who will provide encouragement, accountability, and opportunities to be a part of others' growth process too.

---

[16] Vladas Griskevicius, Robert B. Cialdini and Noah J. Goldstein, "Applying (and Resisting) Peer Influence," *MIT Sloan Management Review* 49, no.2 (Winter 2008): 83-9.

Encouragement

One of the most profound things you can do to maximize your coaching experience is to maximize your interactions with those who will encourage you to learn, grow, and change. People who provide genuine encouragement may be avid supporters of the specific changes you want to make, or they may simply be avid supporters of growth in general—people who are working to improve themselves too. Every time you engage with encouraging people, you'll be reminded that you're not changing because you have to, you're changing because you want to, and you are not alone.

Note that surrounding yourself with support involves limiting your exposure to those who hold you back. People who hinder your progress generally come in one of two forms: they simply reinforce habitual behaviors you now want to leave behind, or worse, they are overly cynical. You may discover that you unconsciously associate certain people with your status quo or your past, and that being around these people now feels like giving up on your goals. The last thing you need when you're investing in your own growth and transformation is to be around those who exhaust you, who scorn your growth, and who doubt your capacity to accomplish your goals.

Accountability

A truly supportive community doesn't let you do whatever you choose—they hold you accountable for doing what you say you'll do. Just as having a workout buddy can help you stay on track at the gym, forming an accountability partnership can be an invaluable tool for sustaining momentum through your coaching activities. Accountability partnerships can take many forms, from informal period meetings to more formal arrangements designed to check in with each other regarding specific goals and action plans.

Reciprocity

Partnering can also be very rewarding when you support someone else through his or her own transformation. Whether or not partners share similar objectives for their respective coaching engagements doesn't matter. Simply meeting from time to time to discuss the growth process can be helpful. You can often double the value of your coaching experience by exposing yourself to the coaching process of your partner.

Application

Make a list of the people with whom you interact on a daily, weekly, and monthly basis. Put a (+) next to each person who has a positive influence on your growth and development, and a (-) next to each person who has a negative influence on your growth. Talk to your coach about how you can limit your exposure to negative influences and maximize your exposure to positive ones.

From the names who have a positive influence on your growth, identify a friend or colleague who you can talk to from time to time about the coaching experience and who might be willing to help hold you accountable to the commitments you make as part of your coaching process.

In forming your partnership, consider discussing the following:

- Overall duration of the partnership, frequency and duration of the interactions.
- Communication protocols (email, phone, text, in-person, etc.).
- What you will and will not hold one another accountable for.
- How you would like to handle situations in which one of you has missed a commitment.
- How you would like to handle changes in the structure of the partnership (timing, style of interaction, etc.).

Tip in Action

When Daniel first went out on his own as a consultant, he realized very quickly that he was surrounded by risk-averse people. Some of them were among his parents, friends, and colleagues. He had to determine who was giving him good advice and who was simply expressing their own fears. It was at this point that he consciously chose to balance the risk-averse influences with the bold attitudes of other entrepreneurs. He joined a networking group for entrepreneurs and began to mindfully avoid talking about his new endeavor to cynical family, friends, and colleagues. As a result, Daniel's social environment became more supportive of his endeavors, giving him more energy, optimism, and courage to move forward.

Section Two:
Maximize Each Session

Each coaching conversation is like a stepping stone toward your goals. To maximize the value of each session:

Tip 11. Come with a Clear Objective
Tip 12. Eliminate Distractions
Tip 13. Take Notes
Tip 14. Take Time to Reflect
Tip 15. Do Your Homework
Tip 16. Translate Insights to Action
Tip 17. Develop New Habits

Tip 11. Come with a Clear Objective

"If you aim at nothing, you will hit it every time"
– Zig Ziglar

In the chapter *Define Success*, we prompted you to define both high-level goals (e.g., strengthening trust) and supporting goals (e.g., improved listening). But to get the most from any given coaching conversation, even a supporting goal, like improved listening, can be too big and too vague. As you prepare for any given coaching conversation, it's helpful to translate these goals into even more specific and timely objectives for your coaching session. An objective for a coaching session clearly states the result you'd like to get out of your time with your coach.

EXAMPLES OF CONVERSATIONAL OBJECTIVES

IF YOUR COACHING GOAL IS TO...	YOUR CONVERSATIONAL OBJECTIVE SHOULD SOUND LIKE...
IMPROVE YOUR LISTENING	Since we last met, I've noticed how often I cut people off and jump in to finish their sentences. I want to hear people out, but I get so impatient with people who say the same thing over and over again. *For today's conversation, I want to learn how to move conversations along without cutting people off.*
STRENGTHEN NEGOTIATION SKILLS	Next week I'm making a pitch to the Senior Leadership Team – asking for $1.5M for a new program that they want me to do with $500K. *For today's conversation, I want to come up with a strategy for getting the entire $1.5M.*

The examples above point to two characteristics of conversational objectives: (1) they clarify what is most difficult for *you* (e.g., based on your personality, experiences, and operating environment), and (2) they connect with real, current challenges.

What About Emerging Challenges?

At times, you may want to dedicate a coaching conversation to something that seems unrelated to your original coaching goals. This often occurs in the context of change—a new boss, an unexpected opportunity for a difficult conversation, a change in market conditions, etc. Whenever you find yourself in uncharted territory, it's an opportunity to leverage your coach: walk through your plans, how you can apply your strengths, and any concerns you have. Nine times out of ten, emergent challenges will present opportunities relevant to your coaching goals, even if you don't see them yet. Don't be so strict about linking coaching conversations to coaching goals that you miss the opportunity to discuss the challenges that are right before you. On the other hand, you're not likely to achieve your coaching goals if you don't prioritize them, so if every conversation is an emergent conversation, it's time to revisit those big-picture goals.

When You Just Don't Know

At times, you may simply not know what you want to get out of a scheduled coaching conversation. When this happens, your conversational objective can be to gain clarity into what you want to focus on. Most coaches are like psychological ninjas in their ability to help you clarify your goals.

Application

Prior to each coaching session, finish this sentence: *"By the end of this coaching conversation, I will be…"*. Share this sentence with your coach, and ask him or her to coach you toward that destination.

Tip in Action

Mike, a senior manager with over thirty years of experience in his field, found it difficult to know what he should get out of any given coaching session. Although he had set clear goals for the coaching engagement as a whole, he often asked his coach, *"What do you think I should get out of today's session?"* Mike's coach sometimes suggested topics, but to Mike's dismay, still asked Mike what a successful outcome of the day's meeting would be. Often, Mike could not articulate what he wanted until the very end of the coaching conversation. Over time, Mike learned what could be accomplished during coaching conversations, and started to come to each session with a specific goal. To his surprise, once he began identifying a goal for each coaching session, Mike discovered that the conversation became more focused and productive.

Tip 12. Eliminate Distractions

"Stop getting distracted by things that have nothing to do with your goals."
– Anonymous

In each coaching conversation (whether formal or on-the-job), you have a limited amount of time to break from the daily grind to explore new ways of thinking and operating. This is a precious time for self-reflection and problem solving. If you allow distractions to sneak—or barge—into coaching sessions, chances are high that you will get less from them.

Research on the brain's functionality when distracted is compelling: distractions reduce productivity,[17] come with "reaction time switching costs,"[18] and create a bottleneck effect in which we may forget important details, like where

---

[17] "Even Small Distractions Derail Productivity," *Association for Psychological Science*, November 10, 2016, http://www.psychologicalscience.org/news/minds-business/even-small-distractions-derail-productivity.html.

[18] Cora M. Dzubak, "Multitasking: The Good, The Bad, and The Unknown," (paper, Penn State-York, 2007), Available from the University of Hawai'i, http://www.hawaii.edu/behavior/306/downloads/Multitasking%20-%20Dzubak.pdf.

we left off in a conversation, or an insight.[19,20,21] If that's not compelling, keep in mind that distractions impact both you and your coach. Trust us: engaging with distractions will detract from the quality of coaching that you receive.

External Distractions

Different people find different environments distracting. For some, the office—even in a local conference room— is rife with distraction. A knock at the door, the sound of conversations going on around you, or inadvertently making eye contact with someone through a glass wall can break your attention at critical moments in the conversation. Such seemingly insignificant events may also, even unconsciously, trigger concern about speaking freely. For others, public spaces such as cafes are no more conducive to the focus and candor that empowers the coaching process. Even if you can't find a perfect setting for your coaching sessions, it's worth taking a few minutes to consider your options and to think creatively about the ideal meeting space.

---

[19] Marcel Adam Just et al., "Interdependence of Nonoverlapping Cortical Systems in Dual Cognitive Tasks," *NeuroImage* 14, no.2 (August 2001): 417-26, 29.

[20] Paul E. Dux et al., "Isolation of a Central Bottleneck of Information Processing With Time-Resolved fMRI," *Neuron* 52 (December 2006): 1109-1120.

[21] Christopher D. Wickens, "Multiple Resources and Mental Workload," *Human Factors* 50, no.3 (June 2008): 449-55.

Internal Distractions

Unfortunately, limiting distractions in your environment may only make you more aware of how distracted you can get from your own thoughts. In his bestseller *Your Brain at Work*, David Rock describes the mind as a stage over which you are the director. Unless you proactively manage your mental stage, it is quite likely that various actors (thoughts, feelings) will jump on stage without warning, creating just as much of a distraction as if an actor was dancing on the table in front of you. When this happens, the trick is to call them your unruly actors and put them in their place. Some of these thoughts may actually be relevant (e.g., your coach made you remember a conversation you want to have) while others may not (e.g., you just remembered it's your partner's birthday tomorrow). To proactively minimize internal distractions, a best practice is to take a few minutes immediately before each coaching session to reflect on your objective for the session (see Tip 5).

When you proactively safeguard against anything that might take your attention away from the coaching conversation, you protect the mental space necessary to participate fully in dialogue with your coach. It's worth the effort.

Application

Create a short checklist of ways that you will create a distraction-free environment during your coaching sessions. Block off five to ten minutes prior to your coaching session to allow time for you to go through the items on your checklist. Checklist items may include:

- Place a Do Not Disturb sign on your office door.
- Let key people know that you'll be unavailable for an hour and give them a special way to reach you only in case of emergency.
- Set your phone to silent, and/or lock it in an office drawer.
- Get something to eat and drink.
- Use the restroom.
- Shut down your computer or move away from it.
- Move to a place you feel free to engage with your coach fully and without reservation.

Here's a test: Go to the space where you're planning to have your coaching conversations. Think of the scariest truth that you could say out loud—something that nearly no one knows. Can you say it out loud, without whispering, in that space? Imagine yourself getting very upset in a conversation. Can you imagine yourself breaking down without worrying about others noticing? If you cannot think of a safe place for your coaching meetings, ask your coach for recommendations.

Tip in Action

Donna's building affords little privacy. There are few walls, fewer doors, and conference rooms with floor-to-ceiling windows. During her initial coaching session, Donna realized that she felt awkward meeting with her coach in a fishbowl conference room. She found herself wondering what her colleagues would ask about her meeting, and she was careful not to express her emotions for fear of being seen by those walking by.

As a result of noticing her own discomfort, Donna started teleworking on the days she had calls with her coach. She made sure that her house would be empty on those days, too. She rescheduled calls on the days that her kids were home from school or her husband was home from work. In addition to feeling more at ease, Donna discovered that she was more capable of gaining perspective on workplace challenges, and could more easily see how her style of managing her organization mirrored her style of managing her relationships with her kids, spouse, and even extended family.

Tip 13. Take Notes

"The faintest ink is more powerful than the strongest memory."
– Chinese proverb

There are all sorts of note-takers in the world, ranging from those who furiously attempt to record every word to those who couldn't find a pen and paper (or other device) if they wanted to. Your personality and preferences will impact your tendency to take notes during your coaching sessions. Rather than defaulting to your personal note-taking preferences, it's worth considering what research says about note-taking, and how it applies to coaching.

The Impact of Note-Taking on Learning

Most note-taking research comes out of the world of education, and shows that note-taking has a significant positive impact on learning and memory, as you tend to remember things that you generate yourself, more so than things others generate for you.[22] In addition, notes can be referenced as a foundation for self-reflection, and self-reflection is a critical pathway for personal growth. But note-taking can also be distracting. Whether you realize it or not, it takes mental energy to take notes—energy that

---

[22] Paul W. Foos, Joseph J. Mora and Sharon Tkacz, "Student Study Techniques and the Generation Effect," *Journal of Educational Psychology* 86, no.4 (1994): 567–576.

may be better invested in thinking further or deeper.[23] In addition, we think and speak far faster than we write or type, so taking the time to record everything that's said in a coaching session may have a dampening effect on the conversation itself. In sum, both research and experience lead us to believe that note-taking should be done with discretion.

What to Record

In our experience both as coaches and as the receivers of thousands of hours of outstanding coaching, it is most helpful to record four aspects of any given coaching conversation: Wins, Opportunities, Insights and Commitments.

- **Wins** reflect progress, and progress is a powerful motivator for growth and continuous improvement.[24] Recording wins helps you to identify them and also to remember them. Memories of success can help you persevere through setbacks.
- **Opportunities** (or if you prefer, **Challenges**)— represent areas for future growth. Recording opportunities is a helpful way to keep track of items that you may want to address with your coach. In our experience, it's quite common for a coaching conversation about Topic A to bring up an opportunity related to Topic B. By recording such opportunities,

---

[23] John P. Rickards et al., "Signaling, Notetaking, and Field Independence-dependence in Text Comprehension and Recall," *Journal of Educational Psychology* 89, no.3 (1997): 508-17.

[24] Teresa Amabile and Steven J. Kramer, "The Power of Small Wins," *Harvard Business Review*, May 2011, http://hbr.org/2011/05/the-power-of-small-wins.

you increase the likelihood that you'll remember to return to them.

- **Insights** represent Eureka! moments—moments when you see things differently and realize that this new way of thinking creates a whole new set of possibilities for you. By definition, insight represents a growth in thinking. Too often, however, insights get lost in the noise of everyday work and life. Recording your insights helps you encode them deeper into your memory, making it more likely that you will remember them and apply them when an opportunity arises.

- **Commitments** represent specific actions or activities that you have promised to do as a result of a given coaching conversation. It's not uncommon for multiple commitments to be generated in any given conversation, and as important as these seem in the moment they can quickly get lost in the mix of other demands on your time and attention. These commitments are important to reference between coaching sessions.

Application

Adopt a strategy for taking notes, including a strategy for making your notes accessible for review. Here are a few common practices:

- Keep a coaching journal. Before each session, write down recent wins and opportunities; after each session, capture insights and commitments. Or just let your mind wander and capture whatever emerges from your stream of consciousness.

- Include Coaching Notes along with other daily notes. Include tabs or other ways to reference outstanding commitments.
- Record Wins, Opportunities, Insights and Commitments separately, such that each reads as a journal unto itself.

Tip in Action

Robert was a self-declared anti-note-taker. In his first coaching session, he commented that writing things down was too much of a distraction for too little value. *"I'd rather look someone in the eye while they talk than be looking down at my notebook,"* Robert stated emphatically.

After acknowledging the value in Robert's decision to prioritize human connection over note-taking, his coach gently challenged several assumptions he was making:
- That his memory was strong enough to capture nuanced details that come from a coaching conversation.
- That he would never want or need to reference something that emerged from a coaching conversation.
- That note-taking would distract him from the conversation.

To Robert's credit, he was open to exploring his assumptions. He quickly realized that he associated note-taking with transcribing—as if notes had to include everything that was said. It had never occurred to Robert that a few bullet points could be quickly jotted down at the end of the conversation. Similarly, once Robert realized that his coach was going to follow up on specific commitments that Robert had made in the course of the conversation, he realized that he needed those bullet points as reminders.

While Robert did have a wonderful memory, the practice of writing down his wins helped Robert to realize that his memory even worked against him sometimes. Robert tended to remember mostly the moments in which he felt he was falling short. Robert began integrating high-level note-taking into not only his coaching conversations, but meetings with his staff and colleagues as well.

Tip 14. Take Time to Reflect

"Try to be the one on whom nothing is lost."
— Henry James

In our experience, most working professionals are strong on action and weaker on reflection—the simple practice of taking time to think about your actions, past, present, and future. You have a million things to do, and you're willing to do one or two more, but to ask you to stop taking action and take time to reflect is like asking you to stop the world from turning. You're so used to *doing* that the concept of *thinking about what you're doing and how you're doing it* seems unproductive; it doesn't feel like making progress. But reflection is absolutely essential for growth.

Reflection Cultivates Growth

Decades of research shows that reflection is an essential ingredient in formulas for growth. According to Kolb's classic learning model,[25] reflection is inherent in two of the four stages of learning. Much has since been written about the centrality of reflection in professional development.[26]

---

[25] David A. Kolb. *Experiential learning: Experience as the source of learning and development* (Vol. 1). (Englewood Cliffs, NJ: Prentice-Hall, 1984).

[26] Jodi Roffey-Barentsen and Richard Malthouse, *Reflective Practice in the Lifelong Learning Sector* (Learning Matters, 2009).

A review of research on reflection in the education sector[27] suggests that reflection enhances the perception of the learner and the relevance of what they're learning; facilitates self-assessment, self-knowledge, use of feedback provided, and self-efficacy; promotes a community approach to learning through sharing with a support community; and ultimately diversifies and improves work practices and performance.

While coaching conversations themselves involve substantial reflection, taking time to reflect outside of your coaching sessions will accelerate your growth. There's a huge difference in progress between a person who only reflects during their coaching sessions and one who reflects before, after, and in the gaps between sessions.

Reflection Strategies

Scott Eblin, author of *The Next Level,* and *Overworked and Overwhelmed,* uses the analogy of the dance floor (action) and the balcony (reflection). This simple framework can help you notice opportunities to move from the dance floor to the balcony. For example, when you're in the middle of an intense discussion, take a moment to switch from being in the discussion to watching the discussion from above (the balcony). Notice your body language, your tone, your use of words. Are they serving you well? What adjustment, big or small, can you try? Just as quickly, switch back to being in the conversation (on the dance floor) and re-engage. The people in the room will never notice.

---

[27] Luminita Drăghicescu, "The Teacher`s Reflective Practice – A Premise Of The Quality Education" (Paper presentation, Edu World 2018, Pitesti, Romania, November 2018).

Another reflective practice is to breathe into insights. True insights are often so powerful that they take your breath away. Consider this phenomenon a gentle reminder to breathe instead of jumping into action. Inhale for 5 seconds and exhale for 5 seconds until the jolt of the insight subsides and your capacity to think deeply returns. This practice of pausing and breathing for a minute or two helps you to think expansively about all the ways to leverage your insight, often highlighting opportunities that you wouldn't have seen otherwise.

Once you find yourself investing in reflection, try adopting The Gibbs Cycle[28] whenever you experience a critical incident.

THE GIBBS CYCLE

---

[28] Graham Gibbs, *Learning by Doing: A guide to teaching and learning methods* (Oxford: Further Education Unit, Oxford Polytechnic, 1988).

In the context of coaching, a critical incident is an event in which you are involved, have the capacity to influence, and care about the outcomes. Critical incidents can provide incredible opportunities for learning, but reflection, not the incident itself, is the teacher. The Gibbs Cycle starts with your description of what happened, then prompts you to record what you were thinking and feeling at the time. Next, evaluate what was good and what was bad about the experience. Based on all of this, record any sense that you can make of the situation; what was going on, not just from a tactical perspective, but also from a people perspective—leadership, influence, power, conflict. Finally turn your attention to yourself. What else could you have done? If this situation happened again, what would you do, or when it does happen again, what will you do?

The Trap of Self-Other Comparison

As you reflect, avoid the trap of comparing yourself (e.g., your growth, your performance, your feedback) to others. Psychologists find that more often than not, self-other comparison is more destructive than constructive. Comparing yourself to someone who you perceive to be better off (more skilled, intelligent, polished, liked, etc.) often elicits negativity and a sense of dejection; comparing yourself to someone you perceive to be worse off (e.g., less skilled, intelligent, polished, liked, etc.) can inflate your ego and prevent you from seeing others' strengths. Or, as psychologist Susan Fiske likes to say, "Envy up, scorn down."[29] Envy, scorn, and the myriad associated emotions (resentment, shame, annoyance, etc.) are all enemies of learning. The trick is to do what psychologists find is a learned behavior of the elderly: compare the current you to the past you.[30] For example, compare what we know now to what we knew then, your current standards to your former standards, your current beliefs to your old beliefs, and your current behavior to your past behavior.

Application

The next time you discover something about yourself that you didn't know before, close your eyes and take a few moments to simply breathe. Inhale. Exhale. Notice how the insight transforms in your mind, becoming more expansive and applicable. Ask yourself a few powerful questions, such as, *"What does this insight do for me?"*, *"How can I leverage this insight today?"*, *"If I really believe this, what will I do next?"* Acknowledge how this insight can create a shift for you; a shift in your standards, beliefs, even in your behavior.

---

[29] Rebecca Webber, "The Comparison Trap," *Psychology Today*, November 7, 2017,
http://www.psychologytoday.com/us/articles/201711/the-comparison-trap.

[30] Mitchell J. Callen, Hyunji Kim and William J. Matthews, "Age Differences in Social Comparison Tendency and Personal Relative Deprivation," *Personality and Individual Differences* 87 (December 2015): 196-9.

Tip in Action

Paul entered into his coaching engagement hoping to learn strategies for molding his senior staff into leaders. He wanted his senior team members to start thinking more strategically. Knowing that Paul could only change himself (e.g., he couldn't change his leadership team), Paul's coach asked him to reflect on his beliefs about each team member. Soon, Paul began to notice how his belief that certain team members were not strategic impacted the way he worked with them. For example, Paul gave certain team members less opportunity to engage in strategic conversations. Paul then began to reflect on his own tendency to judge others too quickly. He began to notice when his mind was more and less open to others' ideas. He also began to catch himself in the judge's seat, and could more quickly redirect his mind back to his own goals and intentions.

Tip 15. Do Your Homework

"Twenty years from now you will be more disappointed by the things you didn't do than by the ones you did."
– H. Jackson Brown, Jr.

In addition to the expectation that you'll take time to reflect before and after coaching sessions, many coaches provide or ask that you co-create homework assignments. Many people associate homework with busywork—worksheets or exercises with little inherent value. But the purpose of homework isn't to keep you busy—it's to strengthen your ability to self-regulate: to motivate yourself, set your own goals, manage your own time, reflect on your own accomplishments, and learn to be your own best teacher.[31]

Homework is leveraged in nearly all learning journeys as a way to boost achievement motivation and to help learners develop the skills to persevere in the face of challenges and setbacks.[32] In the context of coaching, homework is often designed to deepen self-awareness, generate new insights, identify options or solutions, and/or reinforce a new skill.

---

[31] Darshanand Ramdass and Barry L. Zimmerman, "Developing Self-Regulation Skills: The Important Role of Homework," *Journal of Advanced Academics* 22, (February 2011): 194-218.

[32] Janine Bempechat, "The Motivational Benefits of Homework: A Social-Cognitive Perspective," *Theory Into Practice* 43, no.3 (June 2010): 189-196.

As coaches, our observation is that clients who do their homework reach their goals more quickly and create increased bandwidth to cover more and deeper topics.

Ownership

In the context of coaching, your homework isn't the work that was assigned to or asked of you—it's the work that you commit to doing. You need to be discerning in what you agree to. If your coach suggests an exercise that you know you will not do, you can say no. You can also suggest an alternative exercise that you are willing to do. You are most likely to neglect exercises when you are either overwhelmed or underwhelmed by the nature of the exercise you chose or that your coach picked out for you.[33] When you're feeling overwhelmed by what you've committed to do, you can break it into steps and re-commit to one or two of them. When you find yourself motivated only by large, meaningful exercises, you can challenge yourself to do something vastly different or difficult.

Competing Commitments

Even when you co-create your homework and commit to doing it, it can easily be sidelined by all the emerging demands of your job. Your commitment to answering emails, meetings, and work products can compete with your commitment to self-development. When this happens, find ways to do your homework in the context of your work. For example, if you committed to having a difficult conversation that you just don't have time for,

---

[33] Wei Tang and David Kreindler, "Supporting Homework Compliance in Cognitive Behavioural Therapy: Essential Features of Mobile Apps," *JMIR Mental Health* no.2 (June 2017).

look for an opportunity to practice your conversational skills in the context of the meetings you are having.

Doing your homework increases the likelihood that you will put what you learned into use. If you wanted to change your physical posture, would it help for you to sit up straight only during your coaching sessions? Of course not. To achieve lasting improvement in your posture, you would need to bring awareness to your posture and make adjustments many times a day. In the context of coaching, homework is often the practical application of what you're learning.

Application

At the end of each coaching session, be sure that you have one or more homework assignments. Challenge yourself to design your own homework, and be open to the homework your coach assigns. Before these homework assignments get undercut by the demands of daily work and life, identify when and how you will go about completing them. Be sure to take notes as you do your homework, so that you can share not only the outcomes, but also what you learned throughout the process.

Tip in Action

Angelica was so overwhelmed with the demands of her job that she couldn't imagine taking on coaching homework as well. After all, she had reached out to a coach to help reduce her workload, not to arbitrarily increase it. As a result, at the end of her first coaching conversation, Angelica was not prepared for her coach to ask her what she would commit to doing before they met again. *"Honestly, I just need to get my work done,"* Angelica said. *"I can't take on anything more."*

Angelica's coach knew from their conversation how overwhelmed Angelica was feeling. She also knew, however, that Angelica would never escape from her cycle of overwhelm unless she invested in her own growth. Her coach asked Angelica to identify one takeaway from their conversation that she could implement immediately.

Angelica was baffled. Like most of us, Angelica was used to homework being assigned to her, not generated by her. But Angelica's coach just waited for her to respond. Angelica paused and closed her eyes. The coaching conversation revealed how hard it was for Angelica to say 'no.' How could she translate this into homework for herself? Finally she realized that she could simply give herself the assignment of saying 'no.' *"I could identify things that I want to say no to,"* she said.

This was a step in the right direction, but to Angelica's coach, it sounded like a rather ambiguous commitment. Knowing that strong, specific commitments are more likely to produce results, Angelica's coach asked her how many things she wanted to say 'no' to over the next week. *"At least 10,"* Angelica decided.

As a result of her coach's persistence, Angelica walked away from the coaching session, clear that her homework before the next meeting was to identify at least 10 things that she could say 'no' to each week.

Tip 16. Translate Insights to Action

"Insight is cute but action is drop dead gorgeous."
– Hey There, Chelsie

When you maximize coaching sessions, take time to reflect before and after, and do your homework, you will almost certainly generate important insights. Insights, defined as "the act or result of apprehending the true nature of a thing, especially through intuitive understanding,"[34] serve as springboards for growth, but the springboard is rather useless if you don't jump from it. For example, realizing that you are not as influential as you would like to be isn't the same as *being* or *becoming* influential. To become influential, you will have to do something differently. Insights must be translated into action. How might you get started? When it's not clear what action you need to take, we recommend starting with words and intentions.

Using (Different) Words

Much of the time, the first opportunity to take action on an insight is to thoughtfully consider how the insight might change what you say, and/or how you say things. For example, an insight may lead you to say yes to something for which you previously would have said no. Another key word choice involves use of pronouns. Often, insights lead

---

[34] *Merriam-Webster*. s.v. "Insight," Accessed April 28, 2020, http://www.merriam-webster.com/dictionary/insight.

us to change "I" to "we", "mine" to "ours", or "them" to "us." For example, you may realize that you could have more influence by saying *"our challenge"* instead of *"my challenge."* A third way you might shift your words is to shift the tense in which you speak. Some insights, for example, help you move out of past tense into present or future tense. Other insights help you move from future to present tense, or vice-versa. In all of these examples, the precise nature of the shift in your words will be based on the insight you have.

Setting Intentions

Insights will often reveal the ways in which you react to the world. To switch from a reactive stance to a creative stance, in which you decide in advance how you will respond, and take the reaction out of it, try setting intentions. For example, to become more influential you may need to set an intention to gather your thoughts before speaking. The best intentions are memorable, clear, and concise. Many people use mantras—simple sayings like *"Let Go, Let God"* —to remind themselves of an intention. Others choose an object, such as a coin in their pocket or a picture on their screen, as a symbol of their intention.

Thinking & Feeling

Sometimes, an insight is the tip of a much deeper iceberg. When you find yourself unsettled with an insight or unable to do something with it outwardly, do something with the insight in your own head: keep thinking about it and feeling through it.

Get your thoughts out of the hamster wheel of your brain and onto paper: journal; design a new product, service, or prototype; write a white paper, memo, or pitch. Some people (e.g., extroverts) may find that instead of writing out their thoughts, they want to talk out their thoughts. If talking through your insights is helpful for you, this is a great moment to activate your support system. Schedule meetings and have conversations with people who you trust will encourage you, challenge you to think more deeply, and support your growth.

In the domain of feelings, action often equates to feeling your feelings. When insights come in the form of feelings (e.g., a stab of guilt, the bite of shame, buried anger or grief), it's time to move through them. You might also try to release your emotions by engaging in activities that draw them out. For example, boxing is great for releasing anger; running and lifting weights can help release tension; watching sad movies is a great way to release sorrow. If this sounds uncomfortable or even unthinkable, then you probably need lots of support to do it. Here again, you may find your support system invaluable. In most cases however, the fastest way through the feelings is to work with a fantastic therapist. If possible, interview a few professionals until you find one who draws out these emotions.

When you gain an insight during a coaching session, make sure that you leave that session with some action—however small it may be—that represents an opportunity to take action on that insight. Translating insights into action enables you to embody the change that you want for yourself.

Application

Identify one insight that you gained in a recent coaching conversation. Make a list of ways that you can better express this insight through your actions. Share your list with your coach and discuss ways that you can translate this insight into action, starting with easy examples and working your way up to situations in which you would find it difficult, perhaps even a little scary. Notice as it becomes easier and easier to take action.

Tip in Action

Charles, the leader of an international design team, often showed up for coaching sessions visibly off balance. He rocked back and forth in his chair, his eyes darted around the room, and his fingers fidgeted with the papers in front of him. Charles felt himself pulled in all directions, at all times of the day and night. He found it difficult to focus on conversations, both with his coach and with his team. Charles' coach challenged him to adopt a centering practice.

At first Charles struggled—he found sitting still in his chair awkward and unnatural. His coach encouraged him to identify a position of strength and stability that was familiar to him. As an avid cyclist, Charles realized that he was most stable when *in the drops*, perched over the drop bars of his bike, weight in his legs, his feet balanced on the pedals. Charles recognized that he could quickly center himself by recreating this position at this desk. With one foot planted in front of the other, sitting on the edge of his seat with his forearms resting on the desk in front of him, Charles felt as stable as in the saddle of his bicycle.

Tip 17. Develop New Habits

"To thine own self be true."
– *William Shakespeare*

Taking action on your insights is a great first step to growth. But you're not aiming to do something differently just this once; you're aiming to do something differently moving forward. Moreover, you're hoping that over time, this new behavior will become easier and easier, until it's just your new normal. In other words, you're aiming to form a new habit. As you may have realized from past attempts, new habits can be difficult to form. Leveraging the science of behavior change can help.

Cues and Rewards

In *The Power of Habit*, Charles Duhigg summarizes decades of research on the formation of habits. While most habits form unconsciously, it is possible—though difficult—to form new habits. The difficulty lies in the fact that your brain becomes addicted to the habit.

Imagine that you're trying to replace a habit of interrupting people with a new habit of listening deeply. You started with a homework assignment to catch yourself interrupting and to identify the thing that triggered you to do so. In this example, the trigger to interrupt is what Duhigg refers to as a cue—something that sets the habitual behavior in motion. Let's say that your homework assignment helps you recognize two specific cues for interrupting: (1) you have an idea, and (2) you disagree with what is said. When either or both of those things happen, you find yourself habitually speaking over others. Identifying the cue is half the battle. Next you'll need to identify the reward.

Habits become addictive because there is a reward that you crave. To break the addiction, your new habit will need to be equally, or even more, rewarding than the old habit. The reward for interrupting is likely a release of dopamine in your brain, which you experience as a small high associated with a sense of relief—the idea is out of your head and into the conversation. The question now is, how might you experience the same or greater dopamine release from listening instead of interrupting? This is the hurdle to jump if you are to change the habit. In order to experience a dopamine rush from listening, you'll have to experiment with ways of listening until you find one that truly competes with the high of interrupting. New habits are formed when you successfully recreate rewards that equal or outweigh the rewards of the old habits. Until you find a reward for listening that outweighs the reward of jumping in, listening will always feel like a chore.

Using Reminders

In the process of forming a new habit, it can take a while for a new reward to emerge and take hold. During this period of time, you'll need gentle reminders to nudge you out of your old behavior. The best reminders are things that you look at or touch each day. Many people use their calendar. If you use your calendar to remind you to attend meetings, make important calls, pick up the kids, tell someone happy birthday, or remember deadlines, then it's highly likely that your calendar can also be used to remind you to adopt new patterns in behavior. For example, if you're working to reduce your stress level, you might set a reminder to pause and take a couple of deep breaths before and after each meeting.

You might also choose an image or a physical object (e.g., a ring, bracelet, photo, card, or banner across your office wall) that prompts you to act on the new habit you're trying to form. Any object can be transformed into a reminder by the simple act of associating it in your mind with a clear and concise idea or intention. As soon as you say that your wedding band is a reminder to listen, then your wedding band *is* a reminder to listen. Choose reminders carefully: a reminder needs to be felt or seen at the moment you need to be reminded. For example, if you want to engage in a new habit upon rising in the morning, your reminder will need to be right by your bed, or between your bed and the nightstand.

Application

Identify a new habit that would support one of your coaching goals (and perhaps even transform your life!). Identify the cue for this new habit: what will trigger your new habit? Is the trigger something someone says? Is it getting in the car? Getting out of bed? Next, create a way to remind yourself to engage in this new habit until the habit itself becomes rewarding. Add prompts to your calendar or find an item that you declare as a reminder of your new habit. Share these ideas with your coach and your support network, and enroll them in helping you identify the reward for your emerging habit.

Tip in Action

Joyce is a fast-acting, always-on-the-go leader who (sometimes) manages to juggle responsibilities at work, at home, and in her community. Through coaching, Joyce came to realize that the fullness of her calendar was largely a result of her habitual way of scheduling meetings and events without room to breathe between them, sunrise to sunset. Being on the go was thrilling for Joyce, but her habitual calendar-packing had downsides that she now sought to avoid. For example, she wished she had more bandwidth for spontaneous events and opportunities, and now and then a lazy afternoon sounded great too.

Joyce's first step to forming a new habit—a habit she called *Creating Space for Myself*—was to find something that felt as good, if not better, than the rush of a busy life. As she explored what this might be, Joyce realized that something as simple as a moment to breathe and relax felt wonderful. To form this small new habit, Joyce set a chime to play on her phone at 2:00 p.m. daily. This chime was her reminder to take at least one full, relaxing breath, and to ask herself, *"How can I create more space for myself tomorrow?"* These moments of clear-headedness almost always helped Joyce see ways in which she could indeed create clear spaces on her calendar. After a few months of dedicated practice,

Joyce no longer needed the chime. She habitually prioritized her need for downtime, and successfully integrated downtime into her daily rhythm.

Section Three:
Persevere

When you begin shifting your behavior, you can expect pushback and resistance. Even if others support the changes you're making, it's important to realize that you are a part of a much larger system, and systems tend to resist change. Here we address a number of strategies to persevere through the pushback and resistance you're likely to encounter as you make changes to improve yourself:

Tip 18. Explain Your Change

Tip 19. Embrace Discomfort

Tip 20. Rejuvenate

Tip 21. Distinguish Between Failure and Mistake

Tip 22. Be Your Own Coach

Tip 23. Give Yourself Credit

Tip 24. Give Them Time

Tip 25. Measure Impact

Tip 26. Estimate Return on Investment

Tip 18. Explain Your Change

"In the absence of explanation, people will create one for themselves."
- Unknown

As you consider what you might do or say to translate insight into action and/or to begin new habits, it's normal to worry about how others will perceive your change in behavior. These concerns are legitimate—it's your intuition telling you that it's not okay to simply change your behavior without explanation. The human brain craves understanding. When it doesn't know why something is happening, it fills in the gap with assumptions, jumps to conclusions, and in the absence of information, assumes the worst: *"What's wrong with him/her?"*[35] If you shift your behavior without explanation, people around you are likely to assume that something is wrong, when in fact you're trying to do something better. Let's say, for example, you're working to better delegate to your team. If you want this change to be understood and appreciated, you'll need to share what you're doing and why you're doing it.

When and What to Share
With rare exceptions, we encourage you to be open about many parts of your coaching experience: share your coaching goals, share insights, share what you're doing differently, and share why you're trying to make certain

---

[35] Peter M. Senge et al., *The Fifth Discipline Fieldbook,* (Currency, 1994).

changes. Unless you have a really good reason not to share these details, we recommend that you share them. Here are a few examples of things that our clients have said to their boss and/or team:

- I'm learning that I'm operating in the details, when I need to be letting you all [the team] handle those details. So from now on you make the decisions on the floor. I trust you and I'll back you up. If you need my help, come ask, but even then I'll only offer advice. The decision is yours.

- I've always known that I'm an introvert and a private person, but only just realizing how distant that makes me from my colleagues. Although I don't show it, I do care about you, so from now on I'm going to start meetings by asking how you're doing and sharing a little about how things are going for me. I really do want to get to know each of you better.

- Everyone knows that I have a hard time keeping my mouth shut. What you might not know is that I'm really working on being a better listener. So you might notice that I'm taking deep breaths sometimes, or sitting back in my chair. These are just signs that I'm listening more, and doing my best to let you finish before I contribute to the conversation.

You may not want to share your goals and/or behavioral shifts with, for example, a boss (or other power or authority figure) who is deeply biased against you (e.g., who wants you to fail), or an individual who will feel threatened by, and may retaliate against you, for your pursuit of a given goal. In such cases, rather than drastically shifting your behavior without any explanation at all, you can simply blame it on the coaching process.

My Coach Made Me Do It

When you don't feel safe sharing the deeper truth about what you're learning and what you're trying to do differently, you can honestly attribute shifts in your behavior and/or your approach to your coaching engagement. This may sound like:

- My coach asked me to try this approach, so I'm going to try it.
- My coach recommended a framework for our conversation today. Can we give it a try?
- I'm working with my coach on being more structured during staff meetings. So today we're going to try something new.
- My coach is challenging me to listen more deeply and actively. So if it's okay with you, I'm going to ask more questions today than I usually do.
- My coach is teaching me mindfulness, and I find that it really helps me to relax and focus. So today we're going to take 2 minutes to sit and breathe before we jump into our agenda.

Application

Reflect on the changes you are making in your behavior as a result of coaching. Consider how others are responding to these changes. Are there people who might be more understanding and supportive of these changes if they were better aware of the reasoning behind them? If so, talk to your coach about what explanations you might offer to help others understand and be more supportive of the changes you make.

Tip in Action

Tony loves to take on challenges. Unfortunately, midway through his career, Tony's love for challenges led him to take on so many responsibilities that he was working 60 hours a week on projects that no one else wanted to do. Realizing that he was burning out and starting to hold a grudge, Tony's boss recommended he work with a coach.

With the support of his coach, Tony began to experiment with various ways to reduce his workload. For one, in an effort to delegate, he would politely decline the occasional request and sit with the silence when no one else volunteered. Given that his boss supported Tony's efforts to reduce his workload, Tony was quite stunned when his boss expressed concern over Tony's increased disengagement. To Tony, delegating and saying no reflected a purely positive shift in engagement, not disengagement!

This experience helped Tony understand the importance of naming and explaining the changes he was making—not only to his boss, but to peers and staff members as well. Once others understood what Tony was doing and why, they responded with support and enthusiasm.

Tip 19. Embrace Discomfort

"The curious paradox is this—once I accept myself as I am, then I can change."
– Carl Rogers

Much of what you gain from the coaching process depends on your willingness to leave all topics of discussion on the table. Coaching conversations can bring up uncomfortable subjects, and almost everyone has a topic of conversation that they will do everything in their power to avoid. Your reaction to these uncomfortable topics will have a large impact on how much you gain from coaching. Will you allow discomfort to shut you down, or will you learn to work through the discomfort in order to discover what's on the other side? If you work through the discomfort, you're almost sure to find a few hidden reflexes worth changing, and maybe even one dark truth worth accepting.

Hidden Reflexes

Human beings operate largely by reflex, a result of our conditioned behaviors. The coaching process is designed to reveal these behaviors, so that they may be examined. These patterns can be surprising. For example, you may discover aspects of your personality that you wish you could change. Herein lies the beauty: once you can see something, you can change it. Said another way, you cannot change what you cannot see. By bringing hidden aspects of your personality to the surface, you can begin to question their value, given your specific goals and aspirations.

Dark Corners

Dark corners refer to the parts of yourself that you've hidden away in boxes, in hopes that they will be lost and forgotten. You can either reject these unacknowledged parts of yourself and hope they never reappear, or you can accept them. If you'd like to be free from your past, acceptance is key.[36] Acceptance is not resignation, but rather the means by which you take ownership of your story—past, present, and future. When you accept where you have been, how you have acted, and who you have been, you become the author of your story. Your past no longer defines you; it's merely the context in which you get to define yourself.

Emotional Reactions

When you look at hidden reflexes, and certainly when you look into the dark corners of your life, you're sure to release strong emotions. When you allow emotions to rise to the surface rather than avoiding them, you create an opportunity to work with them. It helps to remember that the emotions you experience are not right or wrong, good or bad; they are simply a natural part of growth. Here are a few practical ways to calm an emotional reaction:

- Name it: If you can name a feeling, you can tame that feeling.

---

[36] Denise Fournier, "The Inescapable Importance of Acceptance," *Psychology Today*, November 27, 2017: http://www.psychologytoday.com/us/blog/mindfully-present-fully-alive/201711/the-inescapable-importance-acceptance.

- Put it out there: By acknowledging and communicating your feelings of vulnerability, the judgments of others lose their ability to send you into a spiral of self-condemnation.
- Allow yourself to feel the feeling—it will pass soon enough.
- Schedule time before and after coaching sessions to prepare and to decompress.
- Remind yourself that feelings are a natural part of change.
- Remind yourself of the higher purpose toward which you are working.
- Use a mood shifter: Music, pictures, physical activity, jokes, etc. to help you calm down and focus on all that is good in life.

Improvisation

Another effective response to discomfort is to improvise. Improv—the act of doing something "spontaneously or without preparation"[37]—is especially helpful when you feel stuck. When you don't *know* what to do next, allow yourself to make up what to do next. As an example, consider how music teachers help students learn to manage the discomfort of performing on stage in front of crowds of people. A common approach is to ask students to spend up to half of their practice time playing anything they like, continuously and without stopping. The approach inspires students to move through discomfort and to quiet their inner critic.

---

[37] *Lexico*, s.v. "Improvise," Accessed October 31, 2020, http://www.lexico.com/en/definition/improvise.

Improv is what allows great musicians to keep playing when they hit a dissonant note, rather than stopping dead in their tracks. Similarly, improv is a practice that can allow you to keep talking when you hit on a topic that seems too uncomfortable to discuss. Just open your mouth and see what comes out. Trust yourself to say exactly what needs to be said.

It takes courage to look at unconscious patterns and dark corners in our life, to calm emotional reactions and to improvise your way through the discussion of uncomfortable topics. When you are willing to embrace discomfort, you will increase your likelihood of discovering opportunities for truly transformational growth.

Application

Take a few moments to scan your life, from your earliest memories to your most recent. Which sections do you prefer to skim over? What words would you use to describe this memory? Consider sharing these words with your coach and/or a professional therapist.

Note: In instances where we have experienced trauma or intense pain, we may find that it's only appropriate to address these topics with a professional therapist. Many of us have found that coaching led us to therapy, and many who search through their past with therapy also search for their future with a coach.

Tip in Action

For twenty years, Sharon was a highly accomplished human resources executive. In recent years, she found herself exhausted and overwhelmed by her position. One day, Sharon's coach asked her about her social life. Initially, Sharon resisted this topic, seeing it as irrelevant to her sense of feeling overwhelmed. However, as soon as Sharon was willing to open up to her coach about her life outside of work, she realized that her career had so dominated her life that her friendships had become nonexistent.

Sharon soon realized that she could handle the stress of management more effectively when she invested time in friendships outside of work. Although it was painful to shine a light in this dark corner of her life, Sharon thanked her coach for encouraging her to go there.

Tip 20. Rejuvenate

"Intentional living is the art of making our own choices before others' choices make us."
– Richie Norton

Coaching can be concurrently invigorating and exhausting. If you are actively engaged with your coach, you'll have a lot to think about and a lot to do. You'll have things to reflect on, feedback to revisit, homework to do, new habits to form, a support community to connect with, and nearly constant effort to choose your words and your actions more mindfully. As you form new habits, new neural networks are forming in your brain. Clearly, coaching consumes a huge amount of energy—mentally, emotionally, and physiologically. When you begin to feel too tired to prepare for your next coaching session, too tired to practice that new approach you committed to practicing, and too tired to talk about your growth, it's time to rejuvenate.

Rejuvenation 101

Many people respond to exhaustion through food, drink, and sleep; a cookie, a glass of wine, early to bed. There's nothing wrong with these strategies, until they're the only ones you're practicing. To rejuvenate effectively, you need to address the physiological, emotional, and mental aspects of exhaustion. Consider the list of strategies below:

REJUVINATION STRATEGIES

PHYSIOLOGICAL	EMOTIONAL	MENTAL
✓ Get 8 hours of sleep, regularly ✓ Take a nap ✓ Go to sleep and rise at a consistent time ✓ Eat consistent meals and snacks; if needed, work with a dietician to design a food plan ✓ Drink water (about 2 liters/day) ✓ Exercise ✓ Practice Somatic Awareness (see below)	✓ Make a gratitude list, or say out loud something you're grateful for ✓ Look at pictures and images that make you smile ✓ Infuse a bit of fun and laughter into your day ✓ Read happy news stories ✓ Indulge - take a break for coffee or tea, a walk in the sun, a non-work conversation, a good book, or even a massage.	✓ Start each day with an accomplishment ✓ Declutter your work space ✓ Block off time before and after coaching sessions to clear your mind ✓ Pick up a mindfulness practice (e.g., find a time during the day to do a simple breathing meditation - see below)

A core concept of coaching is that the physiological, emotional, and mental domains must shift *together*, otherwise the unshifted domains will be like anchors that sink your efforts. For example, if you focus only on eating habits without addressing your emotional and mental triggers for poor eating, then you'll always feel like you're on a diet. The only way to make healthy eating feel effortless is to work through the emotional and mental aspects of healthy eating in tandem.

Most of the strategies listed above are well known if not exactly straightforward, but two deserve a deeper dive: Mindfulness and Somatic Awareness.

Mindfulness
The Oxford Dictionary defines mindfulness as "a mental state achieved by focusing one's awareness on the present moment, while calmly acknowledging and accepting one's feelings, thoughts, and bodily sensations, used as a

therapeutic technique."[38] To practice mindfulness, you must first focus on the present moment. This is not easy, because your mind operates in three time zones: past, present, and future. The goal is to filter out those other time zones, so that you can more clearly identify what *is,* be less influenced by what *was,* and not worry about *what will be.*

Perhaps the easiest way to bring your attention to the present moment is to focus on your breath. Breathing is automatic—it's unconscious until you bring your attention to it. When you bring your attention to your breath, you'll find all sorts of interesting, present-moment sensations to pay attention to. Each time you inhale and each time you exhale, tiny little sensations fill your nose, throat, chest, and lungs. When you attempt to focus on these present-moment sensations, you'll begin to notice just how easily your mind wanders, and you'll develop more and more capacity to notice these drifts and bring your mind fully back to your breath.

The impact of just a few minutes of mindfulness a day is remarkable. Although the neurological mechanisms are not fully understood, research has demonstrated that the simple practice of focusing on your breath for a few minutes each day increases happiness, life satisfaction, and goal clarity, and decreases nervousness, tension, anxiety, burnout, anger, and even physiological symptoms of stress

---

[38] *Lexico*, s.v. "Mindfulness," Accessed October 31, 2020, https://www.lexico.com/en/definition/mindfulness.

(e.g., cortisol levels).[39] Now that's what we call rejuvenation!

Somatic Awareness

Mindfulness is the gateway to somatic awareness; the keen sense of what is going on in your body at any given moment in time. Somatic awareness may start with becoming conscious of your breath, but it expands to the tips of your toes and even into the energy field surrounding you. Somatic awareness enables you to pinpoint pain and discomfort in your body, and to move and stretch to relieve it. Somatic awareness enables the effective use of body language to communicate—for the kindness, concern, interest, and passion to feel to be expressed through the way you hold yourself. Somatic Awareness also signals how you feel about people, ideas, opportunities, and challenges.

The body is a wonderful barometer. Subtle shifts in your body (e.g., sensations in your gut, arms, legs, throat, and skin) are the first signs that you are relaxed or anxious, confident or overwhelmed, satisfied or dissatisfied, and so on. If you tune into it, your body can signal whether or not a person, idea, or opportunity really resonates with you. To build your somatic awareness, we strongly recommend picking up an activity that has an explicit mindfulness component, such as martial arts or yoga, and finding an instructor who challenges you to bring attention to your body throughout the activity. The practice of somatic

---

[39] Rollin McCraty, *Science of the Heart: Exploring the Role of the Heart in Human Performance*, (Boulder Creek, CA: HeartMath Institute, 2001 Edition).

awareness is a bit like other forms of exercise. It's exhausting when you're doing it, but invigorating for days to come.

Getting Ahead of Exhaustion

Personal development is much like mountain climbing and distance running. If you wait until you're exhausted to prepare, eat, drink, or give yourself a pep talk, it's probably too late. As mountain climbers and distance runners know all too well, you have to drink before you feel thirsty, eat before you feel hungry, rest before you are too tired to go any further, and think positive thoughts before the negative ones gain a foothold. If you regularly find yourself parched, famished, falling asleep at your desk, and/or battling negative thoughts and feelings, it's time to hit reset and try a new pattern: rejuvenate *before* you feel the need to do so, well before you are exhausted.

Application

Choose at least one physiological, one emotional, and one mental rejuvenation strategy to begin practicing every day, even when you don't think you need it. Leverage the list above or make your own list. Work with your coach to identify the strategy that will serve you best.

Tip in Action

Tara left the office for a walk every day. Olya set aside five minutes to meditate after lunch. Mike parked in a lot several blocks away from his office so that he could walk to and from work. Sylvia came into work an hour late on the days when she had a coaching session. Eric blocked off an hour after each coaching session to walk and reflect on the conversation. Susan filled a large container of water at the beginning of each day and committed to finishing it before dinner. Sara worked with a dietician to fuel her body more consistently. Each of these clients found one way to rejuvenate—a reminder that while they can't fully control their energy, they can take action to manage it.

Tip 21. Distinguish Between Failure and Mistake

"A failure is not always a mistake—it may simply be the best one can do under the circumstances. The real mistake is to stop trying."
– B. F. Skinner

To allow maximum room for growth, consider the distinction between failure and mistakes. Failure is the absence of success; mistakes are actions based on incorrect information or guidance.[40] We often feel that our mistakes equate to failure—that incorrect actions threaten our success—but this is rarely true. In fact, mistakes often lead to great accomplishments. Consider some of the world's most beloved products: bubble wrap was originally marketed as wallpaper; WD-40 got its name from being the 40th attempt at creating a degreaser that worked. Likewise, your greatest achievements are probably riddled with mistakes—things you would have done differently if you had known better. When you differentiate between mistakes and failure, you can deal with these two experiences in vastly different ways.

---

[40] *Lexico*, s.v. "Mistake," "Failure," Accessed October 31, 2020, http://www.lexico.com/en/definition/mistake, http://www.lexico.com/en/definition/failure.

How (Not) to Fail at Coaching

In the domain of coaching, success is your ability to make significant progress towards the goals you set for your coaching engagement. Thus, the way to fail is to not learn, and/or to not change when you know you need to. No one wants to get to the end of their coaching engagement to look back and realize that they didn't learn what they wanted to learn, and they didn't make the changes they wanted to make. To avoid such failure, we strongly recommend revisiting your goals and your progress with your coach at regular intervals. Some people do this at the end of every coaching session; others find that monthly, quarterly, or even a simple mid-point check-in is sufficient.

If at any point you realize that you are failing to accomplish your coaching goals, it's time to dive into deep self-reflection to figure out how you can grow from your coaching experience and what is next for you. Your coach will likely be more than willing to help you think through whatever is stopping you. For example, you may need to better communicate the changes you want to make, or you may need to overcome the negativity of unsupportive people in your life. Sometimes, you may realize that there's something about how your coach works or communicates that is holding you back. If you can describe what you want your coach to do differently, then share it! Most coaches are extremely versatile and can adjust their coaching style when asked. If you find yourself wanting to work with a different coach, yet you cannot clearly articulate why or what you want in a new coach, then we encourage you to dive deeper still: What are your barriers to learning, growing, and changing? What could anyone do or say to help you overcome those barriers? As long as you keep your sights set on the overarching goal of coaching—to learn, grow, and change where change is needed—then failure doesn't have to be an option.

Learning from Mistakes

Mistakes, in the context of coaching, often take the form of dead ends and rabbit trails; seemingly unimportant tangents that don't feel relevant or worthwhile. It's ironic really: to get the most from your coaching experience, you must be willing to explore new ways of thinking and doing. And yet occasionally, a path of exploration will feel like a dead end or a waste of time. This can happen in conversation (e.g., your coach asks questions that don't help you get anywhere) and in action (e.g., you try out a new strategy to influence someone, and it doesn't work). You may also make a mistake in terms of priorities. For example, you might mistakenly focus on one topic or one goal at the detriment of another, or you may neglect to work through the one thing that would really propel you forward.

It's important to realize that these mistakes don't necessarily derail the success of your coaching engagement —and in fact, much like bubble-wrap, they often result in unexpected breakthroughs. If you assume dead ends and rabbit trails are a waste of time, they are certain to be just that. If you stay open to the possibility that mistakes are part and parcel of the larger process of self-inquiry, then you'll discover that they are a necessary part of the adventure.

Application

Reflect and/or journal on the following questions:

- Could you allow for the possibility that this feeling of being stuck is just a feeling and not necessarily a reality?
- How is this apparent dead end an opportunity for action or new ways of thinking?
- How does what you have learned from running into this dead end empower you?

Tip in Action

As the founder of a utilities company, Carina worked hard to build a fantastic team. When the company's new technology translated into rapid growth, however, she found herself as the target of widespread criticism by people who barely knew her. Soon, that criticism seemed to bleed over and color the perceptions of those who had once sung her praises. Frustrated and tired, Carina began working with a coach to take her leadership skills to the next level.

To her credit, Carina jumped in with enthusiasm, openly trying new ways to run her meetings, to respond to emergent problems, and to coach her staff. But with a rapidly growing and diversifying set of stakeholders to lead, there was no way that Carina could meet everyone's needs and desires. Carina had opened a feedback loop that was now overflowing with often contradictory observations and requests. For every person who saw her efforts as authentic, just as many saw them as fake; for every person who craved the changes she was making, just as many wanted something different.

As the excitement of working with her coach wore off, Carina fell into a state of despair, feeling like she was failing everyone, including herself. Fortunately Carina did not hide these feelings of failure from her coach, which allowed the two of them to reframe her experiences as learning opportunities—perhaps mistakes in others eyes, but all part of the growth process. Perhaps more importantly, Carina was able to define true failure. For Carina, failure would be giving up on her ability to lead the company to success. Others' feedback may point out mistakes (improvements that she could make with any given person or team), but corporate metrics such as growth, profit, and employee well-being replaced others' feedback as her gauge of success vs. failure.

Tip 22. Be Your Own Coach

"An ounce of practice is worth a ton of theory."
– Anonymous

One of the primary benefits of coaching versus group training is that the one-on-one attention and support makes it possible for the growth experience to be tailored completely to you. Part of the tailoring is done by your coach. For example, you can expect your coach to adjust their approach to working with you based on many factors, including your goals, personality, and learning style. But even the best coaches need and expect their clients to inform and augment their tailoring efforts. The key to fully tailoring your coaching experience is to be your own coach—to actively participate in crafting your coaching experience. To activate your inner coach, we recommend that you intentionally (1) influence your conversations, (2) allow spillover, and (3) share what you learn.

Influencing Your Conversations

Since the impact of coaching relies heavily on the nature of your conversations with your coach, it's essential for you to positively influence your coaching conversations. The primary ways to influence coaching conversations have already been covered in earlier tips. Here we'll speak to more nuanced ways to influence your coaching conversations. For starters, you don't have to wait for your coach to ask you powerful questions. Nothing is stopping you from reflecting on the questions you know will serve you well, or even telling your coach to ask you a certain question—perhaps one that you are scared to answer out loud. You can also let your coach know how best to challenge you. When your coach offers you a framework, you can share how you might tailor that framework to maximize your challenge and growth. You can even influence your coach's style of working with you: if your coach's approach isn't serving you in some way, you can request an adjustment.

Before moving on, we need to make a very important distinction. Influencing your coach can greatly improve your coaching experience when it's in service to your growth and your learning curve. On the flip side, it's also possible to influence your coach in service to your comfort or reluctance to change. For example, if you suggest questions that are easy for you to answer, if you limit the degree to which you'll allow your coach to challenge you, you'll never step out of your comfort zone. Likewise, if you tailor frameworks to conform with your existing beliefs, or if you customize your homework to fit too closely with your current way of doing things, you'll learn nothing new. Walk this line carefully; a true inner coach will always seek to make you just a little uncomfortable.

Allowing Spillover

In the context of coaching, spillover occurs when the things you're learning in one domain (e.g., professional) spill over into other domains (e.g., personal). For example, what you learn about yourself as a leader can impact the way you parent your children, what you learn about your values and beliefs can inform how you lead, and what you learn about being healthy can influence how you manage your time. When you allow your growth in one domain to spread into other areas, you magnify the impact, and increase the likelihood that new habits will take root. As you achieve your coaching objectives, look at the other areas of your life, and see which may benefit by applying the frameworks, strategies, or habits that you've learned. A powerful way to maximize your return on investment in coaching is to seek out such opportunities to transcend your immediate coaching goals.

Sharing What You Learn

If you're committed to remembering what you're learning through your coaching experience, then you'll find opportunities to share with others. Time and again, studies have demonstrated that teaching is one of the best ways to ensure that what is learned is not forgotten.[41] Research suggests that on a neurological level, sharing what you've learned forces your brain to retrieve the lessons learned from short-term (aka, working) memory.[42] Each time you retrieve an idea or concept from your working memory, it becomes more likely that your brain will consolidate it into

---

[41] Peter A. Cohen, James A. Kulik, Chen-Lin C. Kulik, (1982). "Educational Outcomes of Tutoring: A Meta-analysis of Findings," *American Educational Research Journal* 19, no.2 (January 1982): 237–248.

[42] Christian Jarrett, "Learning By Teaching Others is Extremely Effective - A New Study Tested a Key Reason Why," *Research Digest*, May 4, 2018, http://digest.bps.org.uk/2018/05/04/learning-by-teaching-others-is-extremely-effective-a-new-study-tested-a-key-reason-why/.

long-term memory, where it is rather easily remembered.[43] In other words, repeatedly teaching a certain concept will trigger your brain to store that concept such that it is easily brought to mind when a situation calls on it. Sharing also helps you dig deeper into the concepts you're learning. As a good listener you will almost certainly ask questions that reveal gaps in your own thinking.

As you seek out opportunities to share what you learn, remember that you can share aspects of what you are learning without sharing too many uncomfortable personal details. For example, you can share a question that had a powerful impact on you without any need to go into *how* the question impacted you. Similarly, you can share about a new habit without needing to go into all the details about what your old habits looked like.

The best coaches want their clients to build the capacity to coach themselves. If you're struggling to be your own coach, ask your coach to teach you a bit about how they learned to coach. When you actively participate in crafting your coaching experience, you exponentially increase the capacity for meaningful outcomes.

---

[43] Alison Preston, "How Does Short-Term Memory work in relation to Long-Term Memory?" *Scientific American*, September 26, 2007, http://www.scientificamerican.com/article/experts-short-term-memory-to-long-term/.

Application

Reflect on the two questions below, and share your thoughts with your coach:

- What request(s) might you make of your coach to ensure the process is optimal for you, your personality, and/or your learning style?
- What is one insight you've gained so far through the coaching process? How might this insight be applied in another aspect of your life? With whom could you share this insight?

Tip in Action

Susan, an executive in a fast-paced consulting firm, soon began to find value in the questions her coach asked during their sessions, as well as the silence her coach created for her to think. Following one particularly helpful coaching session, Susan wondered why she didn't take time to think like this outside her coaching conversations. In that moment, she realized that the only thing stopping her from doing so was her own busy schedule, so she began scheduling time to coach herself. During these times, Susan asked herself questions, slowing down when she landed on a good one and reflecting on that question until she gained insight. As a result, Susan began showing up to her coaching sessions with new insights to build on. Susan's coach noticed the shift, and the two agreed that they would dedicate a bit of time each session to helping Susan learn "the art of the question."

Tip 23. Give Yourself Credit

"Of all the things that can boost emotions, motivation, and perceptions during a workday, the single most important is making progress in meaningful work."
– *Teresa Amabile and Steven J. Kramer*

There are times when your coach will do or say something that cascades into a breakthrough moment for you. A coach's question can lead you to reframe a situation. A coach's challenge can trigger a new career trajectory. A coach's observation can change your way of looking at yourself. It's tempting to give your coach the credit for these breakthroughs, but to do so minimizes everything you've done to precipitate them. Breakthroughs are a tipping point event: even when you don't realize it, there's a lot of time and energy invested before you reach that moment in which it all seems clear. While it's nice to acknowledge your coach's role in the process, it's critical to acknowledge the work that you've invested as well. Giving yourself credit for your insights, growth, and wins triggers positive emotions that boost both learning and performance.

The Progress Principle
Through an analysis of daily experiences of knowledge workers, Amabile & Kramer (2011) discovered a

phenomenon they call the Progress Principle.[44] According to the progress principle, progress goes hand in hand with positive emotions—satisfaction, happiness, and motivation. The implication is that when you acknowledge your progress, you'll have more positive energy to take into the next day. In fact, the progress principle suggests that acknowledging even very small breakthroughs (things that may not seem like a breakthrough at all, until you label them as such) may have a positive impact on your energy levels.

The Happiness Advantage

The Happiness Advantage is a principle, based on decades of research in cognitive, behavioral, and neurological psychology, which states that happiness itself is a strong predictor of success. If you are happy, you are more likely to be productive, creative, and resilient—you are more likely to accomplish the goals you set for yourself. Thus, to the extent that acknowledging your success lifts your emotional state, it will also propel you forward to the next accomplishment. Note that the trigger for happiness is the acknowledgement of success, not the success itself. You don't have to wait for others to acknowledge you; you can give yourself that gift.

Consider this: Your coach's question can only help you reframe a situation when you're open to considering it. A coach's challenge can only change your career trajectory when you are ready to change. Your coach's observation

---

[44] Teresa Amabile and Steven Kramer, *The Progress Principle: Using Small Wins to Ignite Joy, Engagement, and Creativity at Work*, (Harvard Business Review Press, 2011).

can only change your way of looking at yourself when you are ready to look at yourself differently. Many things may happen during your coaching engagement, but only because you have prepared your whole life for those things to happen.

Application

At the end of each day, take a moment and thank yourself for the efforts you have made to improve your life, no matter how small. If possible, do this aloud, mentioning each accomplishment one at a time and pausing between each to feel the endorphins that result from doing this. For added benefit, you can do this while looking at yourself in the mirror. Speak to yourself as you would a friend whom you would like to encourage. Here are some examples of language you can use to get started. Be sure to modify the language to best fit your personality.

- I want to take a moment to acknowledge you for _____. Although it may seem small, this action represents movement in a positive direction. Thank you for taking this step.
- I am proud of you for doing _____ today. It will help you achieve your larger objectives by _____.

Tip in Action

Myra sought a coach when she transitioned from academia to a competitive international corporation. Her first months were painfully difficult, and for a time she felt that her coach was the only person with whom she could talk openly. Within a year, Myra learned how to navigate the company's politics, built strong relationships and a profitable new business line, and was promoted. As her coaching engagement came to a close, Myra told her coach that she never could have made it without her. "Do you really think that's true?" her coach asked. "If I never existed, would you not have figured out another way?"

In the moment, Myra laughed and agreed. In the years to follow, Myra discovered the true value of giving herself credit. From time to time, Myra calls upon her coach to talk through an emergent challenge. But these days, Myra shows up with a renewed sense of empowerment. She acknowledges all the things she has done to get to where she is. As she speaks, it's clear that her ability to celebrate even very small wins is precisely the thing that keeps her charging forward.

Tip 24. Give Them Time

"Trust the process. Your time is coming. Just do the work and the results will handle themselves."
— Tony Gaskins

If you follow the tips in this book, you will most assuredly gain much from your coaching engagement. Indeed, you may develop in ways you never thought possible. As coaches, we have worked with mediocre managers who became great managers, poor communicators who became sought-after public speakers, timid individuals who became fearless leaders—the examples go on and on. If you're one of those who gains much from your coaching engagements, you may be disappointed to find that others' perceptions of you don't change as fast as you'd like. Don't take it personally. Others' perceptions of you will always lag behind your reality.

The Influence of Beliefs on Perceptions

The Reflexive Loop, a phenomenon that occurs within the Ladder of Inference,[45] explains why others' perceptions lag behind your reality. As you can see in the graphic, beliefs impact data points.

---

[45] Peter M. Senge et al., *The Fifth Discipline Fieldbook,* (Currency, 1994).

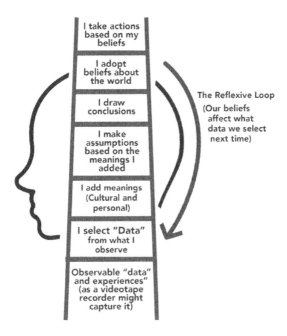

For example, if your boss believes that you are conflict avoidant, they will notice all the data that supports that belief and will tend to filter out evidence to the contrary. This phenomenon occurs independently of the changes you've made to confront conflict more directly. In order for your boss's perception of your conflict style to change, you will need to not only be incredibly consistent in your more direct approach, you will also need to point out your more direct approach to your boss (and any other people whom you want to take notice).

The Importance of Sharing

In Tip 18, we addressed the need to explain the changes you're making and why you're making them. Here we underline this tip and expand it to the whole of your coaching engagement. In addition to being explicit about any given change you're making and why you're making it (e.g., delegating differently), create opportunities to be equally explicit about how you've changed more holistically. For example, explain how your point of view has changed, how your values have shifted, and any new success strategies that you've adopted. Help the people closest to you get to know the upgraded you—the you who thinks a bit differently, feels a bit differently, and acts a bit differently.

Overcoming Fixed Mindsets

Don't be surprised if those around you—particularly those close to you—are unmoved by the shifts you've made over the past months. Research suggests that roughly 40% of people adopt a fixed mindset at any given moment in time, believing that character and abilities are static, genetically programmed, and thus can't change much over time.[46] These people are hard to convince that change, certainly transformational change, is possible. Again, don't take their skepticism personally. Remember all the times when you, too, adopted a fixed mindset. Extend grace, and hold tight to your growth mindset.

Be Your Own Measuring Stick

While others' acknowledgement of the shifts you've made is fantastic confirmation that it's not just all in your head, there will always be people who don't notice or don't want to see you as the next best version of yourself. Do not

---

[46] Carol Dweck. *Mindset: The New Psychology of Success.* Random House, 2006.

allow such blindness or stubbornness to trigger you. When working with those who don't acknowledge the improvements you've made, focus not on their measuring stick, but on your own. First create specific, objective benchmarks that represent the attitudes and behaviors that you are holding yourself to demonstrating. Then do a regular audit of the degree to which you're hitting these personal benchmarks. Whenever you find yourself feeling unfairly judged through the lens of your past, pull out these benchmarks and remind yourself that someone who can't upgrade their opinion of you is not someone whose feedback holds value.

Application

Identify one or two assumptions people make about you that you would like to see shift as a result of coaching. Work with your coach to create a plan for changing these perceptions. In your plan, consider including:

- Honest conversations regarding your coaching goals.
- Behavioral benchmarks of success.
- Requests for accountability partners who know what you're trying to do differently and will point out when you do and don't follow through.
- Feedback partners.
- Check-in meetings with your boss and/or other key stakeholders.

Tip in Action

Robert had developed a reputation as a bull in a china shop, particularly when engaging with managers of other functional units. Rather than sharing ideas and asking his peers what they thought, Robert would declare his plans as indisputable facts; rather than seeking to build consensus among his peers, Robert would move forward regardless of others' opinions. Through coaching, Robert began to realize that while his bullish approach had contributed to his success thus far, it would hold him back from senior management roles. Robert made a sincere commitment to change, and from that point on, he began asking more questions and taking others' perspectives into account.

After a few months of adopting these new behaviors, Robert expected his colleagues to acknowledge him as a collaborative business partner. Instead, Robert's colleagues still described him as bullish and inconsiderate. Rather than attributing Robert's new behaviors to a change in him, they assumed his behavior was an anomaly, or worse, that he would undermine their authority in some other way. For Robert, the challenge was to continue seeking collaborative business relationships even when his colleagues remained wary of him.

Tip 25. Measure Impact

"The measure of success if not whether you have a tough problem to deal with,
but whether it is the same problem you had last year."
– John Foster Dulles

By the end of your coaching engagement, you will have invested significant time and resources in your growth. To what end?

In our experience, clients underestimate the importance of measuring the impact that coaching has had on themselves and others. Furthermore, even those who appreciate the value of measuring impact struggle to figure out how to quantify their progress. The impact of coaching can be measured both qualitatively and quantitatively, from individual impact to corporate impact, with metrics of success based on (but not limited to) the goals of coaching.

Qualitative Measures of Impact

A compelling and straightforward way to measure the impact of your coaching engagement is to collect qualitative data – descriptions of behavior, thoughts, attitudes, and experiences.[47] In the context of coaching, where your goals are typically expressed in terms of shifts in behavior,

---

[47] *APA Dictionary of Psychology*, s.v. "Qualitative Research," Accessed February 15, 2021, https://dictionary.apa.org/qualitative-research.

thoughts, attitudes, and experiences, we recommend collecting open-ended descriptions of the shifts you have made. To design your approach, discuss the following elements with your coach:

- **Input Providers:** To ensure that qualitative data you collect isn't biased in any way, it's critical to gather data from everyone who has had a substantial opportunity to witness the shifts you've made. For example, if you decide that people you interact with at least three times a week should have a substantial opportunity to witness the shifts you've made in your communication style, then you should seek to collect input from everyone that you interact with at least three times per week.

- **Anonymity:** Will anyone in the group you seek input from feel uncomfortable being completely candid? If so, ask for feedback through a platform that provides anonymity, like SurveyMonkey.

- **Response Rate:** When you collect any type of data from people, the validity of the input you gather depends on the response rate. A 100% response rate isn't required nor realistic, but ideally you can get responses from 70 to 80% of those surveyed.

- **Specificity to Your Coaching Goals:** To the extent that you identified and pursued specific goals in the context of your coaching engagement, you should seek specific input related to those goals. Consider the examples below, which build on our previous example of high-level and supporting goals:

QUESTIONS THAT EXPLORE THE IMPACT OF COACHING, BASED ON COACHING GOALS

IF A GOAL OF YOUR COACHING ENGAGEMENT WAS TO:	YOUR REQUEST FOR INPUT MIGHT SOUND LIKE:
Strengthen Trust through: – Improved listening – Greater empathy – More directness – Greater self-awareness	"My primary goal over the past 6 months has been to strengthen trust through improved listening, greater empathy, more directness, and greater self-awareness. Please share the ways in which you've seen me improve in this area, along with the impact that any improvements I've made in this area have had on you, your success, and/or our relationship."
Influence Up, through: – Stronger negotiation skills – Broader perspective-taking – Political savvy	"My second goal over the past 6 months has been to influence up, through stronger negotiation skills, broader perspective-taking, and political savvy. Please share the ways in which you've seen me improve in this area, along with the impact that any improvements I've made in this area have had on you, your success, and/or our relationship."

Quantitative Measures of Impact

In many industries, numbers speak louder than words. If you're working in a data-driven environment, it will serve you well to demonstrate the impact of coaching through quantitative measures in addition to the qualitative input you receive.

Quantitative data is the expression of information numerically, for example through percentages or scale scores.[48] Quantitative data is often everywhere, once you start looking for it. Work with your coach to explore the data that is lurking just beyond your fingertips, and consider the possibilities below.

Difference Scores. One way to demonstrate change over time is via difference scores—literally, the difference between a data point at Time A (e.g., prior to coaching) and

---

[48] *APA Dictionary of Psychology*, s.v. "Quantitative Data," Accessed February 15, 2021, https://dictionary.apa.org/quantitative-data.

Time B (e.g., following coaching). Difference scores that are commonly related to coaching goals may include:

- Changes in your team/organization's engagement scores prior to, and following coaching
- Changes in the frequency in which your ideas were funded/approved
- Changes in performance metrics, e.g., supervisor evaluation, sales, accepted proposals, etc.
- Changes in key relationships, e.g., resolution of conflict, improved communications, reduced tension

Difference scores are fascinating to explore but are often muddied by factors outside of your influence. For example, an increase in your team's engagement scores could reflect your growth, or it could reflect some other change in the work environment that you had nothing to do with.

Look for quantitative data that relates to your coaching goals as closely as possible. For example, you might look at specific items on an employee engagement survey vs. the overall score your group received. To further clarify the extent to which any difference scores can be attributed to the changes you've made, consider asking relevant stakeholders what they perceive to have contributed to the difference in score. This can be done via anonymous, open-ended surveys, focus groups, or interviews, and represents a combination of quantitative and qualitative data.

Direct Measures of Change. As an alternative to looking for difference scores, consider looking for and asking for more direct indicators of change. A direct measure of change is one that speaks to the change itself rather than extrapolating change from a before/after comparison. Direct measures of change are specific by design, typically co-created by coach and client to reflect the client's coaching goals and to collect input from relevant stakeholders.

Building again on our example of high-level and supporting goals, consider the following examples of direct, quantitative measures of change.

EXAMPLE OF DIRECT, QUANTITATIVE MEASURES OF CHANGE

IF A GOAL OF YOUR COACHING ENGAGEMENT WAS TO:	A DIRECT, QUANTITATIVE MEASURE OF CHANGE MIGHT BE:
Strengthen Trust through: ☐ Improved listening ☐ Greater empathy ☐ More directness ☐ Greater self-awareness	Using the scale provided, please rate the degree to which, over the past 9 months, I have: ☐ Improved my listening ☐ Showed greater empathy ☐ Expressed ideas and feedback more directly ☐ Demonstrated greater self-awareness Rating Scale: - 2 = Much worse 0 = Neutral/No change + 2 = Much better

Timing

There is no one perfect time to measure the impact of your coaching. Given that it takes time for others to notice the changes you've made, it's often prudent to wait 3 to 6 months after you've made changes to ask others about them. On the flip side, memories are short. Consider a timeframe that is reasonable to ask others to remember something new or different about your approach. Perhaps most importantly, if you anticipate working with your coach over an extended period of time (6 months or more), consider collecting impact measures along the way, e.g., at the 3-month, 6-month, and 12-month marks.

Keep it Simple

All too often, clients and even their coaches, assume that it's just too difficult to measure the impact of coaching. Indeed, if you approach measuring your progress as a massive, multifaceted effort, you're likely to forego it altogether due to the substantial cost and time required to get it just right. And while it's true that organizations don't always have the budget to fund a robust measurement of coaching impact, that doesn't have to get in the way of more streamlined efforts. If it's a question of whether the impact of coaching will get measured at all, then choose the most simple approach. Choose one or two people who have had the opportunity to witness the changes you've made, and ask them for feedback.

Leveraging Your Findings

Perhaps the reason that so few clients make the effort to measure impact is that they don't know what they would do with impact data if they had it. In fact, there are a large number of high-impact ways that impact data can be leveraged. Consider the following:

- Use data collected throughout your coaching engagement to inform both your approach and your goals.
- Share your wins with others as encouragement for them to give coaching a try.
- Share the data you collected with your Talent and HR team to help them build their case for investing in coaching more broadly.
- Use your data to inform your own journey. What do you want to work on next?

-   Share your wins with your coach, who can use your story (anonymously or not, per your agreement) as encouragement for others.

Application

In collaboration with your coach, identify a potential set of quantitative and qualitative measures of the changes you've made, relevant to your coaching goals. As you brainstorm together, consider these questions:

-   What impact would you hope or expect the changes you've made to have on your team, your relationships, your organization, or organizational outcomes?
-   Which of your performance metrics would you hope or expect to be impacted by the changes you've made?
-   What data is available, even if it's not typically referenced as a performance metric?
-   What other data is collected in your organization that may reflect the changes you've made through coaching?

Tip in Action

William was a member of the CXO team of a rapid growth company which invested heavily in coaching for the entire senior leadership team. William in particular viewed coaching as a valuable resource and sought to leverage his coach as much as possible.

After working with his coach for 4 months and making a number of substantial shifts in the way that he delegated problem-solving, managed meetings and supported his team, William asked his coach to interview his team to collect their input. Together, William and his coach devised a set of interview questions that would provide qualitative measures of change, including:

"William has been working on trusting you and other members of the team to generate great solutions to everyday problems. Tell me what's different about his approach when the team encounters a problem."

The result of this early check-in was a rich set of examples of how William's team appreciated his new approach. As one might expect, team members also pointed out that when William was particularly stressed, he was more likely to slip back into his old habit of monopolizing their problem-solving process with his own ideas. The nuances that emerged from these interviews reinforced the value of his new approach, and also reinforced the need for him to work on his reactions to stress.

Toward the end of his coaching engagement, William and his coach repeated the interview process. The second set of questions were different from the first, some reflecting on the overall change that his team and other stakeholders had observed over the past year, and some reflecting more specific changes that he had made over the past six months. William again used the narratives collected to inform his goals moving forward, but this time he also shared a summary of the narratives with his Talent team and with his coach, so that they could leverage his story as a testimony of the power of coaching.

140

About three months later, William gained access to another year's worth of employee engagement data. Although the overall corporate numbers had ups and downs, he was pleased to see that among his own leadership, responses to three items that directly related to his coaching goals increased by more than 10 points.

Tip 26. Estimate Return on Investment

"Twitter is like hugging. Just because it's hard to measure the return on investment doesn't mean there isn't value there."
-- Tony Hsieh

Just like Twitter, the return on investment (ROI) of coaching is extremely difficult to measure. And yet, knowing that any measurement will be flawed, it is far from an exercise in futility. In contrast, the process of determining the ROI of your coaching engagement is as fulfilling as the result. Consider this: the combined qualitative and quantitative measures of your impact are only one small factor in the equation. It's fascinating to consider all the other benefits that were achieved for you, your team, and your organization as a ripple effect of coaching.

To estimate the ROI of your coaching engagement, consider this formula:[49]

$$\text{Return on Investment of Coaching} = \frac{(\text{Benefits Achieved} - \text{Coaching Costs})}{\text{Coaching Costs}} \times 100$$

Each element of this equation can be further broken down into their own formulas.

---

[49] Nadine Greiner, "Executive Coaching: An ROI Sample Calculation," *Association for Talent Development*, October 16, 2018, Accessed February 15, 2021, https://www.td.org/insights/executive-coaching-an-roi-sample-calculation

Estimating Benefits Achieved

To calculate the financial value of benefits achieved through coaching, identify relevant elements from the list below, add your own elements, calculate estimated financial value for each element, and add these numbers together.

BENEFITS OF COACHING, IN DOLLARS

BENEFITS TO:	SAMPLE CALCULATION

☐ Your own increased engagement	Consider the shift in your own Productivity Index:
	  – Actively Disengaged: 50% productive
	  – Somewhat Disengaged: 66% productive
	  – Engaged: 100% productive
	  – Actively Engaged: 150% productive
	Convert this to dollars by multiplying your salary by the Productivity Index corresponding to your level of engagement (B) before and (A) after coaching, then subtract B from A to estimate the financial value of increased engagement.

☐ Others' engagement	Repeat the process above for each person whose engagement has improved as a result of your coaching
☐ Efficiency of processes, meetings, etc.	Estimate the number of hours that you save yourself as a result of coaching per week. Take this weekly number, and multiply it by your hourly pay (salary / 2080 hours if you work 40 hours/week), then multiply by 52 for an estimated annual cost savings. Repeat this step for members of your team who are more efficient as a result of the changes you've made through coaching.
☐ Sales	Amount of revenue that you attribute to coaching.
☐ Customer retention	Earnings from repeat business that you attribute to coaching.
☐ Production of new products or services	Value of the product or service you or your team produced as a result of coaching.
☐ Your decision to stay with your organization	50 - 75% of your annual compensation (more if your position is hard to recruit for, less if it's easier to recruit for).
☐ Others' decision to stay with the organization	50 - 75% of the total annual compensation of team members who would have left the organization if you had not received coaching.
☐ Reduced stress	Employees who report high levels of stress have health costs that are 150% of moderate to low-stress employees. As of 2019, the average cost of healthcare per person in the US was $11,582. Significant reductions in stress save organizations about $5,800 per year per employee.

Estimating Executive Coaching Costs

To calculate the total financial cost of coaching, consider the elements below. For each relevant element, calculate estimated costs and add these costs together.

COST OF COACHING, IN DOLLARS

COST OF:	SAMPLE CALCULATION
☐ Finding your coach	Estimate the number of hours that your Talent/HR team invested in locating your coach. If you're not sure, ask. Then convert this to dollars by multiplying team members' hourly pay by the number of hours invested.
☐ Your coaching engagement	The total dollar amount of your coaching engagement.
☐ Coaching tools and resources	The total dollar amount of any tools or resources not included in the cost of your coaching engagement—perhaps even this book!
☐ Collecting feedback and input from peers, etc.	The number of hours that your team, peers, and management team invested in providing input to you and your coach, e.g., via 360 completion, interviews, etc.

Crunching the Numbers

There is no perfect science to calculating the ROI of coaching. Once you've brainstormed and collected all the relevant numbers that you and your coach can think of, plug them into the Return on Investment of Coaching equation above and prepare to be shocked. If you've evolved your mindset and your approach in meaningful ways, chances are high that the magnitude of your Returns greatly outweighs your Investments. If you've evolved your mindset but not your approach, you may be shocked to find that there is still work to be done to justify the Investments you've made in coaching. Either way, the reflection and calculations that go into calculating ROI are extremely valuable.

Application

As you near the end of your coaching engagement, work with your coach to identify the many benefits that have emerged along the way. Use the examples above as a starting point, but don't be limited by them. Embrace the imperfection of this process—don't let perfect be the enemy of good and helpful. Instead, do your best to put dollar amounts to the benefits you identify. Then estimate your coaching investment, calculate ROI and share with your coach:

- How do you feel about this ROI? Did you hope for more, or anticipate something less?
- Who could benefit from hearing about your ROI?
- How can the ROI you experienced serve others in your organization or community?
- How can the ROI you experience serve your coach, through the lens of their continuous development and/or through the lens of this business development?

Tip in Action

Tina had come to coaching ready to resign from her role as an administrative officer, a role she had been successful in for over 10 years. Her growing dissatisfaction stemmed largely from a conflict with a new member of the leadership team, who treated her with great disrespect and attacked her work in public settings. Tina felt that she couldn't win and didn't have the power or poise to stand up for herself without coming across as defensive. As a result of the verbal abuse, she had completely disengaged

145

from the leadership team and was looking for a new employer.

As a result of a six-month coaching engagement in which she invested 12 hours of her time, others invested about 10 hours of time to complete her Leadership 360 survey, and her organization invested $10,500 in coaching costs, Tina:

- Decided to stay in her role, as a result of her success in forming a pleasant and respectful working relationship with this leader;
- Actively re-engaged with the leadership team;
- Adopted a daily gratitude practice which reduced her stress and improved her interactions with family;
- Learned to stand up for herself and her work in a polite but firm way.

Based on this list of immediate results, Tina and her coach calculated benefits achieved and cost of coaching as follows:

Benefits Achieved, in Dollars:

Tina's decision to stay with the organization, estimated at 50% of her annual salary of $140,000: *$70,000*

\+

Tina's shift in engagement, from disengaged to actively engaged, estimated at ($140,000*1.5) - ($140,000*.66):

$117,600

\+

Significant reduction of daily stress level: *$5,800*

=

Total Benefits of Coaching: $193,400

Cost of Coaching:

12 hours of Tina's time @ $130/hour: *$1,560*

$+$

10 hours for 360 @ and average of $125/hour: *$1,250*

$+$

Cost of Coaching, including 360 survey: *$10,500*

$=$

Total Cost of Coaching: $13,310

Plugging these numbers into our equation for ROI, they discovered:

$$\text{Return on Investment of Coaching} = \frac{\left(\$193,400 - \$13,310 \right)}{\$13,310} \times 100 = 1,353\%$$

Tina was stunned…both by the magnitude of ROI and by the fact that this number did not even reflect the priceless ROI of gaining the ability to stand up for herself and her work.

Applying These Principles to Everyday Life

The objective of this book was simple: to empower you with actionable guidance that helps you work smarter, not harder, to achieve breakthrough results both personally and professionally. By beginning coaching engagements with clearly articulated goals, a willingness to look openly and honestly at any obstacles that may exist, and orchestrating a supportive environment, clients can grease the wheels on their personal and professional development initiatives.

While the tips in this book have been presented within the context of coaching, they are useful in any transformational endeavor. Far beyond the context of coaching, this book serves as a useful and timely reminder of proven principles that make the change process easier. The tips you have read are applicable to any endeavor you might undertake to advance, learn, and grow.

We hope that you will return to this book time and time again. Allow the tips herein to serve as reminders and tangible strategies for owning and taking responsibility for the intentions you set, the actions you take, and the results you experience. If you continually lean into the concepts in this book, you will strengthen and expand your growth muscles and empower yourself to achieve success beyond your wildest dreams.

Bibliography

Amabile, Teresa, and Steven J. Kramer. "The Power of Small Wins." *Harvard Business Review*, May 2011, http://hbr.org/2011/05/the-power-of-small-wins.

Amabile, Teresa, and Steven Kramer. *The Progress Principle: Using Small Wins to Ignite Joy, Engagement, and Creativity at Work*. Harvard Business Review Press, 2011.

Bempechat, Janine. "The Motivational Benefits of Homework: A Social-Cognitive Perspective." *Theory Into Practice* 43, no.3 (June 2010): 189-196.

Bridgeland, David M., and Ron Zahavi. *Business Modeling: A Practical Guide to Realizing Business Value*. Burlington: Morgan Kaufmann Publishers, 2018.

Casanova, James, Ken Day, Denice Dorpat, Bryan Hendricks, Luann Theis and Shirley Wiesman. "Nurse-Physician Work Relations and Role Expectations." *JONA: The Journal of Nursing Administration* 37, no.2 (February 2007): 68-70.

Callen, Mitchell J., Hyunji Kim and William J. Matthews. "Age Differences in Social Comparison Tendency and Personal Relative Deprivation." *Personality and Individual Differences* 87 (December 2015): 196-9.

Cohen, Peter, James A. Kulik and Chen-Lin C. Kulik. "Educational Outcomes of Tutoring: A Meta-analysis of Findings." *American Educational Research Journal* 19, no.2 (January 1982): 237–248.

Corley, Tom. *Change Your Habits, Change Your Life: Strategies that Transformed 177 Average People into Self-Made Millionaires.* Minneapolis: North Loop Books, 2016.

Dalton, Amy, and Stephen Spiller. "Too Much of a Good Thing: The Benefits of Implementation Intentions Depend on the Number of Goals." *Journal of Consumer Research* 39, no.3 (October 2012): 600-14.

Drăghicescu, Luminita. "The Teacher`s Reflective Practice – A Premise Of The Quality Education." Paper presentation, Edu World 2018, Pitesti, Romania, November 2018.

Dux, Paul E., Jason Ivanoff, Christopher L. Asplund and René Marois. "Isolation of a Central Bottleneck of Information Processing With Time-Resolved fMRI." *Neuron* 52 (December 2006): 1109-1120.

Dzubak, Cora M. "Multitasking: The Good, The Bad, and The Unknown." (paper, Penn State-York, 2007), Available from the University of Hawai'i, http://www.hawaii.edu/behavior/306/downloads/Multitasking%20-%20Dzubak.pdf.

Foos, Paul W., Joseph J. Mora and Sharon Tkacz. "Student Study Techniques and the Generation Effect." *Journal of Educational Psychology* 86, no.4 (1994): 567–576.

Fournier, Denise. "The Inescapable Importance of Acceptance." *Psychology Today*, November 27, 2017, http://www.psychologytoday.com/us/blog/mindfully-present-fully-alive/201711/the-inescapable-importance-acceptance.

Gibbs, Graham. *Learning by Doing: A guide to teaching and learning methods.* Oxford: Further Education Unit, Oxford Polytechnic, 1988.

Gourville, John T., and Dilip Soman. "Pricing and the Psychology of Consumption." *Harvard Business Review*, (September 2002), http://hbr.org/2002/09/pricing-and-the-psychology-of-consumption.

Greiner, Nadine., "Executive Coaching: An ROI Sample Calculation," *Association for Talent Development*, October 16, 2018, Accessed February 15, 2021, https://www.td.org/insights/executive-coaching-an-roi-sample-calculation

Griskevicius, Vladas, Robert B. Cialdini and Noah J. Goldstein. "Applying (and Resisting) Peer Influence." *MIT Sloan Management Review* 49, no.2 (Winter 2008): 83-9.

Jarrett, Christian. "Learning By Teaching Others is Extremely Effective - A New Study Tested a Key Reason Why." *Research Digest*, May 4, 2018, http://digest.bps.org.uk/2018/05/04/learning-by-teaching-others-is-extremely-effective-a-new-study-tested-a-key-reason-why/.

Just, Marcel Adam, Patricia A. Carpenter, Timothy A. Keller, Lisa Emery, Holly Zajac and Keith R. Thulborn. "Interdependence of Nonoverlapping Cortical Systems in Dual Cognitive Tasks." *NeuroImage* 14, no.2 (August 2001): 417-26, 29.

Kolb, David A. *Experiential learning: Experience as the source of learning and development* (Vol. 1). Englewood Cliffs, NJ: Prentice-Hall, 1984.

Ladd, Kimberly S. "The Experiences of Students Who Increased Curiosity During Their First Year of College: A Grounded Theory Study." *Dissertation Abstracts International Section A: Humanities and Social Sciences* 80, (2019): 3-A(E).

Mayberry, Matt. "The Extraordinary Power of Visualizing Your Success." *Business Insider,* February 14, 2015, http://www.businessinsider.com/the-extraordinary-power-of-visualizing-your-success-2015-2.

McCraty, Rollin. *Science of the Heart: Exploring the Role of the Heart in Human Performance.* Boulder Creek, CA: HeartMath Institute, 2001 Edition.

Pillay, Srinivasan. "The Science of Visualization: Maximizing Your Brain's Potential During The Recession." *HuffPost,* November 17, 2011, http://www.huffpost.com/static/about-us.

Preston, Alison. "How Does Short-Term Memory work in relation to Long-Term Memory?" *Scientific American*, September 26, 2007, http://www.scientificamerican.com/article/experts-short-term-memory-to-long-term/.

Ramdass, Darshanand, and Barry L. Zimmerman. "Developing Self-Regulation Skills: The Important Role of Homework." *Journal of Advanced Academics* 22, (February 2011): 194-218.

Rickards, John P., Brett R. Fajen, James F. Sullivan and Gerald Gillespie. "Signaling, Notetaking, and Field Independence-dependence in Text Comprehension and Recall." *Journal of Educational Psychology* 89, no.3 (1997): 508-17.

Roffey-Barentsen, Jodi, and Richard Malthouse. *Reflective Practice in the Lifelong Learning Sector*. Learning Matters, 2009.

Schacter, Daniel L., Donna Rose Addis, Demis Hassabis, Victoria C. Martin, R. Nathan Spreng and Karl K. Szpunar. "The Future of Memory: Remembering, Imagining, and the Brain." *PubMed Central*, (November 2013): http://www.ncbi.nlm.nih.gov/pmc/articles/PMC3815616/.

Senge, Peter M., Art Kleiner, Charlotte Roberts, Richard B. Ross and Bryan J. Smith. *The Fifth Discipline Fieldbook*. Currency, 1994.

Shin, Dajung Diane, and Sun-il Kim. "Homo Curious: Curious or Interested?" *Educational Psychological Review* 31, no.4 (December 2019): 853-74, http://doi.org/10.1007/s10648-019-09497-x.

Taibbi, Christopher. "Brain Basics, Part One: The Power of Visualization." *Psychology Today*, November 4, 2012, http://www.psychologytoday.com/us/blog/gifted-ed-guru/201211/brain-basics-part-one-the-power-visualization.

Tang, Wei, and David Kreindler. "Supporting Homework Compliance in Cognitive Behavioural Therapy: Essential Features of Mobile Apps." *JMIR Mental Health* no.2 (June 2017).

U.S. Department of Health and Human Services, Centers for Medicare and Medicaid Services, *National Health Expenditures 2019 Highlights*, Accessed February 15, 2021, https://www.cms.gov/files/document/highlights.pdf.

U.S. Department of Health and Human Services, Public Health Service, Centers for Disease Control and Prevention, National Institute for Occupational Safety and Health, *Stress at Work*. Ohio, 1999, DHHS (NIOSH) Publication No. 99-101, https://www.cdc.gov/niosh/docs/99-101/.

Webber, Rebecca. "The Comparison Trap." *Psychology Today*, November 7, 2017, http://www.psychologytoday.com/us/articles/201711/the-comparison-trap.

Wickens, Christopher D. "Multiple Resources and Mental Workload." *Human Factors* 50, no.3 (June 2008): 449-55.

Acknowledgements

We extend our sincere gratitude to Don Rheem for contributing such an excellent Foreword to this 2nd edition of The Coaching Companion; to Pat Mathews, Chalmers Brothers, Brandon Moreno and Richard Godfrey for their glowing and humbling endorsements; to Erin Greenwell for her outstanding editorial work; and above all, to a God whose grace and unconditional love fills us up so that we can serve this world.

Cary would also like to thank John Keyser, whose insistence that she start writing after many years of complacency led to this work; her husband, Ben, who told her to go "write" while he tackled a million other things; and her son, Charlie, whose energy and enthusiasm make it impossible for the demands of writing a book to stand in the way of the most important things in life.

Daniel would like to thank his parents, Richard and Jo, for being as much friends as they are inspirations. Daniel would also like to thank the following individuals among his many personal coaches and mentors, Chetan Prakash, Alicia Rodriguez, Anabel Suarez, Sameer Sharma, Juhl Valecourt, and his writing partner Cary—her infinite energy and creativity inspires him to no end.

About the Authors

Carylynn Larson

Carylynn (Cary) Kemp Larson is an Organizational Psychologist and an IFC-accredited leadership coach based near Washington, DC. Cary combines deep scientific expertise in the social sciences with extensive C-suite coaching  and consulting experience to elevate even the most successful leaders. Cary's clients describe her as brilliantly insightful, pragmatically blunt, and contagiously positive. She has a knack for knowing which frameworks and resources will profoundly impact her clients. Cary helps her clients activate new awareness and heighten conversational, relational, and emotional capacities. Cary is herself an entrepreneur and community leader, founding a national non-profit and serving as its Executive Director, and currently, President.

On a personal note

I have deep compassion for what my clients go through on the receiving end of the coaching engagement. It is hard to be coached. Coaching can be draining. That said, is through the experience of being drained that we allow ourselves to be filled up with something new, something more than the muck that drained out.

When Daniel shared the idea for the 1st edition of this book with me, I was astounded that such a book didn't already exist. Given the investment that individuals and organizations make in coaching, and the impact that coaching can have at individual, team, and organizational levels, it just makes sense to give our clients every resource at our disposal to help them get the most out of their coaching engagement.

In the past, I would have thought to myself, *"I wish I could do something like that"* and responded, *"Great idea – let me know how it turns out!"* But this time was different. My own coach had helped me recognize my worth and make bold offers and requests, and I was only a little surprised to find myself asking, *"Can I co-author that with you?"* Since the publication of that first edition, I've made many more such bold offers and requests, each opening a new door.

Each of us has encountered at least one shift that can change the trajectory of our life. Coaching helps us discover what is possible; it helps us start to see the fruits of the shifts we make in leadership and in life.

Daniel Sheres

Daniel Sheres is a leadership coach and organizational development consultant based in Washington, D.C. In addition to coaching senior executives, he is actively engaged in the development of organizational cultures that support and sustain effective leadership at every level. Daniel's approach supports leaders to better understand both the internal drivers and external context for engaging successful leadership behaviors. Working from within the client's most pressing leadership challenges, his coaching supports the ability to perceive and navigate complex situations, communicate effectively, delegate with authority, and to demonstrate resilience and resourcefulness through transition. An avid Aikido practitioner, he teaches nationally on martial arts principles and their use in executive development to corporate executives.

On a personal note

My own journey into coaching began as a client. I hired my first coach in 2007 to help me build my consulting business. Like many budding entrepreneurs, I had the skill to do the work, but didn't really understand how to win the work. I had a colleague who had worked with a coach and highly recommended it.

Before the first session, I remember expecting my coach to act a lot like a consultant, anticipating that he would ask me questions about my services and strategy and then advise me on what to do. To my surprise, the first conversations weren't about the business at all, but about what motivated me. Initially, I played along, trusting the process as best I could. As we began to get into the details of my professional objectives, I started to see the link between my inner motivators and goals, and the skills and behaviors I would need to develop to achieve those goals. Together we created a plan—and while I would be able to lean on my coach for support and guidance throughout the process, I knew that nothing would change without a sincere commitment from me.

I dedicated several hours each day to reading and practicing new behaviors. I learned how to market myself, negotiate deals, and set and achieve financial targets. I clarified my offers, honed my strengths, and identified the weaknesses that I would have to either develop or delegate. It was a transformative experience, to say the least; by the end of six months I had nearly tripled my income and had a backlog of work extending out almost a year. My fascination with the process of transformation quickly became a passion as I continued working with my coach for another year. Quite naturally, I found myself integrating coaching into my consulting roles, and six months later I began offering coaching as a service.

A qualified coach is only half the equation. The value a client receives from the coaching process is largely dependent on the client's willingness to fully engage in the process. As in many endeavors, it's not about working harder, but rather working smarter. It is my sincere hope that the advice presented in this book will help clients of all coaches realize the full value of their coaching engagement and achieve results well beyond what they initially thought possible.

Additional Resources

We are continuously designing resources to support your ability to get the most from your coaching experience. Upon publication, our Resource Center includes the following, with new resources being added upon request:

- Coach Interview Guide
- Sample Coaching Agreement
- Know, Wonder, Learn Reflection
- Expand Your Circle of Influence Activity
- Explore the Depths of Your Circle Activity
- Guide to Selecting a 360
- Guide to Selecting 360 Participants
- Goal Hierarchy Worksheet
- Visualization Exercise
- Critical Incident Reflection Guide
- Measure Impact: Design Your Feedback Request
- ROI Calculation Worksheet

Please see www.coaching-companion.com/resources.
Use the code 157981 for discounted access.

Made in the USA
Middletown, DE
05 April 2021